Paul
Thank you
Encouraging
Advice

BONDING OF WARRIORS
TRUE STORIES OF THE 9TH DIVISION LRRP / RANGERS
Told by the Brave Men that Lived Them

COMPILED BY
BOB HERNANDEZ

Copyright © 2014 Bob Hernandez.

All rights reserved. No part of this book may be reproduced, stored, or transmitted by any means—whether auditory, graphic, mechanical, or electronic—without written permission of both publisher and author, except in the case of brief excerpts used in critical articles and reviews. Unauthorized reproduction of any part of this work is illegal and is punishable by law.

ISBN: 978-1-4834-1097-5 (sc)
ISBN: 978-1-4834-1096-8 (e)

Because of the dynamic nature of the Internet, any web addresses or links contained in this book may have changed since publication and may no longer be valid. The views expressed in this work are solely those of the author and do not necessarily reflect the views of the publisher, and the publisher hereby disclaims any responsibility for them.

Any people depicted in stock imagery provided by Thinkstock are models, and such images are being used for illustrative purposes only.
Certain stock imagery © Thinkstock.

Lulu Publishing Services rev. date: 7/28/2014

DEDICATED TO THOSE THAT GAVE ALL:

LYNN LEROY MILES JANUARY 29, 1967	ROBERT LOEHLIEN SEPTEMBER 25, 1968	WARREN LIZZOTTE FEBRUARY 18, 1969
KENNETH LANCASTER JANUARY 3, 1968	HERB DONG CHO SEPTEMBER 25, 1968	LONNIE D EVANS APRIL 1969
THOMAS HODGE JANUARY 24, 1968	RONALD MOORE NOVEMBER 4, 1968	MICHAEL VOLHEIM MAY 29, 1969
GEORGE HOUSE JANUARY 24, 1968	JOSEPH CASTAGNA DECEMBER 21, 1968	CURTIS RAY DANIELS MAY 29, 1969
WILLIAM PIASKOWSKI MARCH 14, 1968	RICHARD BELLWOOD JANUARY 25, 1969	HERBERT FROST JUNE 21, 1969
JOSEPH MELVIN JONES APRIL 16, 1968	ROMAN GALE MASON JANUARY 27, 1969	JOHNATHAN LAMB FEBRUARY 11, 1969
JOHNSTON DUNLOP APRIL 16, 1968	LEON DAVID MOORE JANUARY 27, 1969	ROBERT BRYAN JULY 31, 1970
HERBERT VAUGHN MAY 25, 1968	RICHARD THOMPSON JANUARY 27, 1969	MARK TOSCHICK AUGUST 11, 1970
JAMES DILLARD SEPTEMBER 23, 1968	IRWIN EDELMAN FEBRUARY 18, 1969	TRAY VAN NHO 1972

DIED FROM WOUNDS RECEIVED IN VIETNAM
RAY M GALLARDO, FEBRUARY 8, 1972

The person in the photo is the late E Company Ranger Mike Kentes. The photo was taken at the opening day celebration of the "Vietnam Memorial" in 1982. Mike is holding a red carnation to the names of American nurses killed during the war. Mike passed away December 8, 2011 and is buried in Arlington National Cemetery. The Photo was taken by photographer Nick Sebastian and was the cover page of "National Geographic" magazine for May 1985.

FORWORD

Thanks to all those who have put so much effort into sharing their experiences in Vietnam. A very special thanks to Roy Barley, Ralph Harter, Bruce Sartwell, Rick Ehrler, Greg Nizialek, Roy Nelson and Mike Kentes, who made the impossible happen and reunited our unit.

PREFACE

"We are not statesmen; our story is not meant to find answers about why the United States fought in Vietnam. Rather, what we hope to convey to the readers of this book is the message that we were a band of gallant warriors who contributed some of our finest hours for our county. We fought a noble fight with skill and dignity; in the process, we demonstrated our love for America, the American people, and especially the comrades who served alongside of us. That is all the nation can ask of its soldiers."

CLANCY MATSUDA
COMMANDING OFFICER
APRIL 1967 - FEBRUARY 1968

PROLOGUE

"LRRPs in Vietnam, like the SEALs, Rangers, and Special Forces were pound for pound the gutsiest soldiers we had there"

COLONEL DAVID H HACKWORTH

The 9th Division long range patrol was formed at Fort Riley Kansas in the fall of 1966 and deployed to Vietnam in January 1967. The unit was one of 13 LRRP units deployed to Vietnam during the course of the war. The five man teams operated deep in enemy territory often without support of any kind. Acting as the eyes and ears of their units, they faced overwhelming odds. They performed reconnaissance, surveillance, target acquisition and specialty type combat missions.

During January 1968, the 9th Division LRRPs began joint operations with the Navy SEALs to gain training and experience in the Mekong Delta. The missions designated as SEAL-ECHO were highly selective patrols.

On 1 February 1969 the department of the Army formally recognized the 9th Division LRRPs as E Company 75th Rangers. The Rangers were trained to operate in 6-12 man team, and were successful in small ambushes and in defending themselves even when heavily outnumbered by enemy forces.

They were hated, feared and respected by the enemy, and often referred to as "the men with painted faces," Special teams were often sent from North Vietnam to hunt them. Rewards up to $2500 were offered for the body of a single LRRP at a time when the average citizen worked for about 85 cents a day. It was the same bounty for an American Colonel.

Considered to be one of the deadliest units in Vietnam the Rangers continued to take the fight to the enemy applying undeviating pressure against the Viet Cong havens and their supply lanes. The LRRP/Rangers had a great psychological impact on the enemy attacking then in their own back yard until the unit was deactivated in November 1970.

CONTENTS

1) Introduction by Clancy Matsuda xvii
2) The Early Years by Rick Stetson 1
3) Christmas 1967 by Roy Barley 52
4) Kennth Ray Lancaster "Mia" by Tony Hanlon 65
5) "1968" compiled by Hilan Jones 67
6) "Raiders from the Sky" by Pescott "Puck" Smith 97
7) The Shit House Fire by Roy Barley 113
8) General Ewell's Laundry by Dan Bien 121
9) Delta Ranger Employ Charlies Tactics by Jack Bick 125
10) "1969" compiled by Bill Cheek 132
11) "1970" compiled by Brent Gulick 149
12) Recollections of a LRRP First Sergeant by Roy D Nelson 160
13) After Vietnam By Roy Barley 165
14) LRRP/Rangers Company Commanders 173
15) Ranger Creed 175
16) Glossary 177

INTRODUCTION

BY

CLANCY MATSUDA

In July 1993, I was on a flight to attend the first reunion of company E, 50th Infantry (Airborne) 75th Rangers, the elite Long Range Patrol Company of the 9th Infantry Division during the Vietnam War. Sitting next to me was an amiable gentleman who struck up a conversation by asking where I was going. Conditioned by years of experience not to speak to civilians about my wartime service in Vietnam, I was reluctant to tell him the purpose of my trip. He prodded me, and I soon found myself talking excitedly about E Company and my old comrades in arms. It had been over 25 years since I commanded the unit. I told him that I had not seen any of my fellow soldiers since then. The antiwar sentiments that emerged from the war had discouraged us from keeping in touch, but finally a few remarkable resourceful troopers planned our first reunion and made it happen. The businessman listened attentively and asked many questions about my experiences: as it turned out, we had a wonderful conversation. When we landed and were about to part ways, he told me earnestly, "Tell the guys at your reunion thanks from a U.S. citizen." I shook his hand warmly and thought to myself how far the nation had come in finally acknowledging the sacrifices of the soldiers who fought in Vietnam.

Our subsequent reunions have been special times of fellowship. We have become a family of old soldiers, bonded with memories of our common experiences in service to our nation. After our latest reunion in July of 2001, Jack Delaney, one of the gallant warriors of 1967- 68 eras, spoke of somehow recording those memories before they fade too dimly into the mist of a lengthening past. Grievously, this highly admired soldier passed away on May 7 2002; we had just started our history- recording journey. Jack provided the poignant vision for this volume, but it was the men of E Company who made the vision a reality. We invited them to contribute to the writing of our history by sharing their wartime stories with us. Many of them accepted despite having to carve out the time from their busy schedules to do so. We discovered that our memories during the past three decades had indeed faded in certain areas. However, the essence of our adventure remains intact.

How was it that we were so profoundly changed by a war halfway around the globe? The war in Vietnam--the longest in American History--was an outgrowth of the Cold War. During this period of tension between the United States and the Union of Soviet Republics, it was our government's policy to support any nation threatened by Communism. South Vietnam, after its creation in 1954, appeared to be such a nation. It was fighting insurgency supported by Ho Chi Minh, the Communist leader in North Vietnam, whose goal was to unite the two Vietnams through civil war. Americans viewed South Vietnam as a "domino" whose fall would encourage Communist aggression elsewhere in the world. Accordingly, the United States sent military advisers to assist the government of South Vietnam in its struggle against the North. The job was anything but easy. Whereas the government of South Vietnam was weak and corrupt, the North Vietnamese proved far more skilled, dedicated, and resilient than we had expected.

In August 1964, Congress passed the Tonkin Gulf Resolution at the prompting of President Lyndon B. Johnson. This resolution invested Johnson with virtually unlimited power to wage War against the Communists in Vietnam. The following year he committed the first of the major forces to fight there. Dismally, there was no clear U.S. strategy for winning from the start. Preoccupied with his "Great Society" agenda at home, He was unwilling to divert the resources- military, economic, and political necessary to wage the war effectively. He deployed follow-on forces to Vietnam piecemeal and in too few numbers to be successful. Moreover, he and his top advisers tried their best to deceive the American public about the prospects for victory. Johnson hoped that the North Vietnamese leaders would be awed into submission by the escalating and destructive efforts of American firepower; paradoxically, the Viet Cong and North Vietnam Army responded with determination. The fundamental dissonance of American policy at the highest level had tragic consequences for the men who had to execute it on the battlefield.

Although the number of U.S. troops in Vietnam grew to almost half a million from 1965 thought 1967, the overall military campaign was inconclusive. A major turning point occurred in January 1968 with the onset of the Tet Offensive. A major turning point conducted bold attacks against South Vietnam cities and towns; for a short time, they occupied the grounds of the U.S. embassy in Saigon. The majority of Americans at home were shocked and outraged; they had up to now believed that the War was going well. It did not matter that the Viet Cong ultimately failed in their offensive and suffered enormous losses. American casualties remained high and the public realized the victory in Vietnam was not imminent. With his Vietnam policy in shambles and support for the war crumbling, Johnson decided not to run for re-election.

Richard M. Nixon won the presidential election of 1968. Within a few months, a gradual withdrawal of American troops was ordered. Nixon's "Vietnamization" policy succeeded in reducing the number of U.S. troops, but much hard fighting remained. After an invasion of Cambodia to eliminate enemy sanctuaries in April 1970, antiwar demonstrations in the United States grew increasingly strident. Tensions grew worse following the tragic shooting of student demonstrators at Kent State University in May and the adverse publicity surrounding the convictions in the My Lai court martial early the following year. Even Vietnam veterans like John Kerry, who later joined an Organization called "Vietnam Veterans against the War" and testified before the Senate Foreign Relations Committee in April 1971 to express the group's opposition. Antiwar protestors vigorously projected their loss of faith in their government, and they directed their frustration and anger increasingly at the military. The war finally ended for the United States in March 1973, following an agreement between the two sides in January. Nonetheless, the civil war in Vietnam continued. For the next two years, the North built up its power in the South in preparation for a final offensive that came in early 1975. A North Vietnamese victory was assured when Congress refused to provide direct military assistance to South Vietnam despite the entreaties of President Gerald Ford. Americans had enough of the war in Vietnam; even the specter of a Communist victory could not change their minds.

For those soldiers who faithfully answered the call to military service, returning home from Vietnam was full of painful and bitter memories. Antiwar radicals vilified them as mindless automatons and evil executors of a corrupt national policy. They labeled veterans as "baby killers" and spit at them as they traveled home in uniform. These insults were tormenting to the men who went to Vietnam intent on doing their duty and expecting the support of their nation. They tucked away the whole experience in the deep compartments of their minds for many years.

The saga of E Company began unfolding long before the disappointing outcome of the war could be discerned. On February 1, 1966, the 9th Infantry Division was activated at Fort Riley, Kansas under the command of Major General George S. Eckhart. The division trained for ten months and then began its deployment to Vietnam in December. While at Fort Riley, Kansas, the Rangers of E Company approached their training with a sober diligence born of the knowledge that they soon would test their combat skills in the crucible of war. In both training and combat, they did their job magnificently. I consider myself blessed and honored to have been associated with them. Their shining examples of courage, competence, and selfless service will forever obliterate in my mind the shadow that the Vietnam War cast on the national psyche. Many of those examples will be evident in the pages that follow.

Together we faced chaotic and near-death situations, but these challenges brought out the best in our spirit. Our shared experience made us more than just friends and follow soldiers. Something amazing happened in the process of sharing the unique experience of training, fighting, and facing death together-we bonded like brothers. Despite the constant adversity, nothing seemed impossible when one had the support of warrior brothers on every side. Thus, it was that the war in Vietnam became a defining experience in the lives of E Company soldiers.

In the past few years I have read with interest about the exploits of the Ranger and special operations units in a variety of conflicts: World War II, Korean and the Vietnam wars, Iran hostage rescue mission, Grenada and Panama operations, the Gulf War, battle for Mogadishu and the current war in Afghanistan. In reading their stories, I have been drawn to the ethos that is common to all American commandos. They cherish the values of honor, valor, tenacity, teamwork, sacrifice, discipline, loyalty, steadfastness, and selflessness. While they focus on the mission and are oblivious to danger and death during battle, they maintain an incredibly strong commitment to each other. Rangers would not think of leaving a buddy behind--no one is more important to them than their comrades. In every conflict, they have acquitted themselves well because of their devotion to the mission and each other. A phenomenon that results from these priorities is the special bonding among the combatants into a unique brotherhood that carries on for a lifetime.

The men of Co. E can rest assured that they have upheld the proud traditions of their Ranger brothers of other eras. Admittedly there have been times when I viewed with envy the exploits of the Rangers during World War 11 and other conflicts that the nation enthusiastically supported; it is tempting to wish that we had been born into a different era. However, those choices are not ours to make. We must do our duty the best we can when called.

Our story is not about perfect human beings carrying out our duties without flaw. We made mistakes; we had our weak moments; we made decisions and did things which we wish we could have changed; we lived by the code of "kill or be killed." Ours was a lifestyle, which involved a mixture of reckless abandonment, combat proficiency, and teamwork under perilous situations.

Because of the unpopularity of the war, our impulse to renew the bonds of brotherhood laid dormant for two decades after we returned home from Vietnam. Many Americans wanted to purge the war from their memories, but the Rangers of E Company vowed that we would never forget. Our reunions rekindled the spirit of camaraderie; they have become a special time and a place where we have been reminded of the role that our families played in giving us strength to endure and the love to console. We and our fallen comrades have been blessed with wives, children, parents, brothers, sisters, nieces, and nephews who serve as a community to whom our sacrifices and experiences matter. Combatants in war and combat veterans after the war yearn subconsciously for solidarity.

Reflecting on the American experience in Vietnam, former Secretary of State Henry Kissinger called it "an appalling conducted war; an American disaster; self-inflicted; and unnecessary." We are not statesmen; our story is not meant to find answers about why the United States fought in Vietnam. Rather, what we hope to convey to the readers of this book is the message that we were a band of gallant warriors who contributed some of our finest hours for our country. We fought a noble fight with skill and dignity; in the process, we demonstrated our love for America, the American people, and especially the comrades who served alongside of us. That is all the nation can ask of its soldiers.

THE EARLY YEARS

BY

RICK STETSON

The 9th Division was the first Army unit to be organized and trained for overseas deployment to a combat theater since W. W. 11. When the 9th Division was activated at Fort Bragg, North Carolina on August 1, 1942. The Division had over two years to train before being sent to North Africa in November 1942. In 1966, only seven months would pass from the time the first soldiers arrived for basic training to when the first division units would arrive in a combat zone, and just one year from activation, the entire 9th Division would move from Fort Riley Kansas to the Republic of Vietnam.

The Army used the draft to provide the privates needed to fill the newly activated 9th Infantry Division. The critical need was for non-commissioned officers (NCOs) and officers and many were assigned from units in Europe and Korea. To meet the increased need for platoon leaders (2nd lieutenants) the Army had the Infantry Officers Candidate School (OCS) at Fort Benning Georgia.

During the 3rd week of October lieutenants Rick Stetson and Edwin Garrison were handpicked (both were Airborne and Ranger qualified) to help create a new unit for the Division called the Long Range Patrol Detachment (LRPD). Similar units were operating with success in Vietnam and had enhanced the intelligence gathering capabilities of American units. They were instructed to begin an immediate search for volunteers and that the unit would undergo training in Panama at the

Jungle Warfare School before departing for Vietnam. The two officers had to move fast to recruit new members as the unit was schedule to depart for the "Jungle Expert School" in Panama on November 16. Only volunteers were to be interviewed and selected but due to the limited amount of time the officers would have to accept just about any soldier willing to volunteer.

When the word went out for volunteers, Dave Moss joined out of Lt. Ed Garrison's former platoon in C Company, 4/39th. Tom Lindly was an artilleryman and heard about the Long Range Patrol from his first sergeant in the 11th Artillery. His job was to deliver artillery rounds and since his ammunition section had the most men, he was told to submit three names as candidates for the LRRPs. He was the only one from his unit to volunteer so he typed his own transfer request and hand carried it to the acting battery commander, then to the battalion commander, and up to division where it was approved. Lindly joined the Army in 1956 and had more time and grade than most volunteers for the unit. He was one of the few who did not possess an infantry military occupational skill (MOS). Mike Patrick graduated in the top of the Jungle School Warfare class and was one of the first LRRPs to receive the Combat Infantry Badge (CIB). Bob Hernandez was a meat cutter before being drafted and would prove to be one of the early top team leaders. Ray Hulin was a cowboy from Texas and one of the first to make enemy contact.

When the interviews were completed, Stetson and Garrison selected 34 volunteers from a cross section of the 9th Division: 11 were from the 39th Infantry, 10 from the 47th Infantry, 9 from the 60th Infantry, and 2 from the artillery, 1 from the signal battalion and 1 from the 9th Administration Company.

On November 17th two Long Range Patrol officers and 44 enlisted soldiers (11 were members of D Troop's aero rifle platoon) boarded a plane for a trip to Charleston Air Force Base. They were scheduled to depart on November 19th for Panama.

The men had worked hard in Panama and the school provided a realistic idea of what to expect when they arrived in Vietnam. Upon returning to Fort Riley 14 of the men decided to ask for reassignment back to their original units.

1ST Lt. Garrison had helped to instill a "can do" spirit among the original members of the long range patrol. When the unit returned from Panama, Garrison suggested the unit needed a distinctive look and decide on the black beret. With the permission of 1ST Lt. Stetson, Garrison designed a flash and had it produced at a local tailor shop. The berets were an instant hit with the men who caused double takes wherever they went on post.

Captain James Tedrick took command of the unit in Dec. 1966 and deployed ahead of the unit with the advance party. The rest of the unit soon followed.

When the patrol members arrived at Bearcat, they found the base camp to be a flurry of activity. Buildings were being constructed and the noise level during the day was constant. The hammering and sawing of construction crews, vehicles, especially the clanking sound produced by the tracks of tanks and personnel carriers, and always the "whop, whop, whop" of the helicopters taking off and coming in for landings. The men were housed in general purpose tents, while the three officers shared a small general purpose tent. The noon meals were C-rations and some of the boxes had dates going back to 1945. Hot and uncomfortable during the day, the living quarters became livable during the night when the temperatures dropped.

The day after arriving in country half of the men went to Na Trang to attend the MACV "Recondo School," said to be the toughest school in the Army. The three week course tested mental and physical endurance. Special Forces provided the instruction and the final exam consisted of conducting a combat patrol deep in enemy territory. The student's day began at 0500 with a 7-1/2 mile march while carry a weapon; full combat gear and a backpack containing a 30 pound sandbag. The march, conducted in one hour and 15 minutes, was followed by two rope climbs up a 30' rope ladder with the trips down a knotted rope. After breakfast, training was conducted for subjects such as first aid where students learned how to give shots and take blood, map reading, land navigation, and extraction using a McGuire Rig (a long rope with a seat at the end that could hold three soldiers at a time as they swing high over the countryside while moving at a speed of 90 knots). With half the members in Na Trang, the rest of the members began to experience operations in the field.

A mission was handed down for a patrol to perform overnight observation of a nearby road. The men walked out from their bivouac position and soon found the dirt road leading to a nearby village. The area was relatively open without a lot of concealment, but the patrol did the best they could. A curfew was in effect and traffic was not to be on the road at night. In the middle of the night several members of the patrol were awakened by the sound of a man moving near their position. It was as if someone had stumbled upon the position by accident and was trying to move out of there as fast as possible. The remaining hours of darkness were spent in apprehension that the person would return with company but nothing further was heard. At first light, the patrol moved back to the safety of the armored cavalry's position.

The second such mission on 29 January the long range patrol would suffer its first casualty. The team consisted of team leader Sergeant Lynn Miles, point man Bob Hernandez, Bill Hass, John Cox and Lawrence Coonrod. First Sergeant Philip Ponserella also accompanied the team to the field.

A Troop 3/5 Cav had been attacked by a platoon sized element while acting as security for a troop withdrawal during the closing days of Operation Colby in the jungle near Phuoc Tuy. A Troop took the fight to the enemy, but the enemy broke contact and disappeared into the jungle. A troop found itself short on fuel, and the mission was for the LRRPs to ride shotgun on two APC's (armored personnel carriers) while they pulled a trailer of fuel out to them. The LRRPs and First Sgt. Ponserella manned the 60- caliber machine guns on the APC's and headed out into the jungle.

Once in the perimeter the team was ordered to conduct a patrol to search for the enemy. First Sergeant Ponseralla stayed back in the perimeter to monitor the radio. The team found a very large base camp about 1000 meters out, but it was deserted at the time. The team observed a large, freshly dug trench running from west to east. Fresh dirt lined both sides, with a pick and shovel lying on the bottom. They must have just missed the VC as a camp fire was still smoldering. Clothes were hanging from lines tied from tree to tree and small tables were fashioned from tree branches. The team jumped the trench and took a quick recon of the camp before returning to the perimeter.

As late afternoon was approaching, the team again was ordered to go out but this time to set up as a listening post. Night was coming fast and the late afternoon shadows caught the team in a thin part of the jungle without proper cover. It was too risky to keep moving in the dark, so the team set up with little cover. Everything was quite until about 7pm. The jungle seemed to come alive with activity. The team could see lanterns and flash lights coming towards them from all sides. Voices were getting closer and Sergeant Miles whispered into the radio for instructions. Moments later Miles leaned over to Hernandez and whispered in his ear "Their all around us! When I say go, throw a "C.S." (Gas) grenade fire one magazine and get back to the perimeter!! Pass it on to Cox and back to me." Hernandez passed it on and got ready. Moments later, Miles yelled "GO!!" and all hell broke loose!!

Hernandez tossed his grenade, fired a magazine killing a VC only a few feet in front of him. It was then that he made a big mistake! Instead of getting up and running back; he tried to reload his M-16 and he felt Sgt. Miles run by him! Still in the seated position he felt Cox getting up to run too!! When the team opened up on the VC the whole perimeter opened up and tracers were flying everywhere. The noise was deafening as the night was filled with the sound of automatic machine gun fire and the VC yelling and screaming! The team caught them completely by surprise. Hernandez was up and running now trying to find the rest of the team. He tried to stay as low as he could because the tracers were still flying in all directions. The only light was coming from the tracers and he was stumbling and tripping and fell into a small tree. Not sure of the right direction to go, he plowed into a VC soldier and both fell to the ground. Both men just looked at each other and ran in opposite directions. At this point Hernandez had no idea if he was going in the right direction. He dropped to his knees next to a small tree and tried to figure out which direction to run. Then it came to him, the luminous dial on his compass. He pulled out the compass that was tied to the button hole of his shirt and reversed the azimuth.

The automatic fire was still filling the night with tracers but he was able to head in the right direction. After five minutes or so of stumbling through the jungle he heard a voice calling his name. It was Sergeant Miles! He made his way to the voice and Sergeant Miles said he was with Cox but had not seen Hass or Coonrod. Miles told him to stay put and try and find Hass and Coonrod while he called in a sit-rep. Hernandez called out for Hass and Coonrod and soon got a response from Hass. He was not injured and had not seen Coonrod. Miles came back and said that they were going to go back into the perimeter. One of the tanks turned on a flood light and one by one the team ran in as fast as they could. The light when off and they gathered behind one of the APC's. About five minutes or so later someone spotted movement at the point that the team had re-entered the perimeter. The spot light was turned back on and there was Coonrod! He had been hit and was barely able to stand. He was quickly brought in and the light when off.

Soon after Coonrod was dusted off Sergeant Miles told Cox to call in a situation report back to the members of the long range patrol who were monitoring a radio. Cox went up the tank to use the radio, but was turned away by one of the tankers. Sergeant Miles climbed up and took the handset from the tanker and at that instant, a Rocket Propelled Grenade (RPG) round hit him in the chest, Miles was killed instantly.

The VC continued to pour automatic rifle fire and RPG rounds into the Cavalry's position and the tankers returned with a heavy volume of fire. A chill went through the members of the long range patrol who were monitoring the radios. They heard the cavalry spell out the phonetic spelling for the first KIA of the LRRPs, "Mike India, Lima Echo, Sierra." The fire fight lasted into the night as A Troop took more casualties. Sgt Ponserella was lived at the loss of Sergeant Miles. Long Range Patrols were not designed to be used as listening post for friendly units and he was upset that Captain Tedrick had allowed the patrol to be given such a mission.

The long range patrol was designed to operate as their name indicated, at a long range and deep into enemy territory. It was determined that since the long range patrols would be inserted and extracted deep in enemy territory, a close working relationship with an aviation unit was essential. The decision was made to attach the 9th Division Long Range Patrol to D Troop 3/5 Cavalry.

The Cavalry received their aircraft and was fully operational by March 1, 1967. Major William Kahler commanded D Troop, 3/5 Cavalry. The aviation unit consisted of an Areo-scout platoon with five U14-ID Hayes, 10 aviators, 10 crew chiefs and 10 door gunners; an areo weapons platoon with l-OUH-IC aircraft armed with XX-21 and M-5 weapons systems (mini guns and grenade launchers) 20 pilots, plus a crew chief, door gunners and mechanics; a headquarters section and an organic infantry platoon with 1 officer and 41 enlisted soldiers.

In March 1967, a soldier who helped contribute greatly to the reputation and success of the unit joined the 9th Division Long Range Patrol. Master Sergeant Roy Nelson had been the operations NCO for the 3/5 Cavalry when the unit arrived in Vietnam. When the Cavalry supported the 1st Infantry Division as part of Operation Junction City, Nelson had a disagreement with the Squadron commander and he was assigned to the LRRPs after the battle of Bau Bang. Nelson's impact on the long range patrol was immediate, although he was not a typical first sergeant. He was the consummate NCO, always looking after his men and always seeing they had everything necessary to be successful in the field.

He volunteered for as many missions as possible, wanting to observe his young patrol leaders in action. He was instrumental in helping to weed out those not qualified to lead under combat conditions. His goal was to teach the basic skills of survival to every LRRP who joined the unit. He stressed education, fitness and discipline. Nelson's reminder to his men was not to get injured by "doing something stupid." Nelson's first mission was to take five men and guard a 01-E Bird Dog observation airplane that had gone down on a road leading to Long Binh. The night was uneventful and the next day a Chinook helicopter flew in and lifted the airplane out. It was a miss-use of LRRP assets but Nelson had successfully completed the first of many missions and demonstrated he was a first sergeant who wanted to be leading his men in the field, instead of from behind a desk. He would go on to lead some of the first long range patrols to operate in the Plain of Reeds and on Thoi San Island in the Mekong Delta.

On August 21, of 1967 Master Sergeant Nelson led a team in the area south of Xuan loc that resulted in the discovery of a massive VC base camp. The mission demonstrated the ability of the LRRPs to contribute information about the enemy to the division. The team included Sergeant Howard Munn; Specialist Four Tom Kloak; Specialist Hilan Jones and Jerry Fairweather.

On the third day of the patrol in a heavy monsoon rain, the team discovered newly excavated trenches leading to reinforced bunkers. It was the beginning construction of a massive VC base camp. Under the cover of the heavy rain the team moved from bunker to bunker and discovered a couple of tunnels. Point man Tom Kloak entered one tunnel to discover a large underground rice cache; large enough to feed dozens of NVA soldiers. The whole system probably covered an area 300 meters by 500 meters. Nelson knew that because the patrol had gone two nights without any radio relay, and with the enemy all around, considerable caution would be called for as they moved through the tall elephant grass. Sergeant Nelson quickly plotted the location of the base camp on his map and the team moved out to an area known as JFK (because of its size) for extraction.

At the G-2 debriefing the team was questioned about what they had discovered. A rear echelon major said, "You LRRP's are always bringing in bull-shit like this. There is no one out there! The first Brigade just swept through that AO."

Master Sergeant Nelson was quick to speak out: "Sir," I'll bet my stripes on it!" The major asked, "How many you got Sergeant?"

"Six." Sir. I'm Master Sergeant Roy Nelson, the LRRP Company First Sergeant!" "How could you be sure of your location when you had not received a single location fix during the two and a half days you were out there? Sir, "I always know where I am. I have never erred on a location during any of the Long Range Patrols that I have completed! (Nelson was the only person to ace the USAEUR map test while stationed in Germany.)

Nelson quickly drew-up detailed maps of the NVA base camp while a B-52 Arc-Light (a B-52 air strike) was diverted from a target in 1lCorps to the target area. Immediately after the air-strike, elements of the 11th Armored Cavalry, along with the 2/39th Infantry Battalion swept back through the area. For the next three days they made contact with the enemy at least thirty times and discovered more than seventy bodies as a result of the air strike. Thirty three more enemy soldiers were killed during the sweep. Also captured was thirteen A-K 47's, RPG rocket launchers; 7.62mm machine gun; seventy two grenades, over eleven thousand rounds of assorted small arms ammo, a mortar tube, miscellaneous rocket and mortar tubes, miscellaneous rocket and mortar rounds, two base plates for 60mm mortars a bipod for an 81mm mortar, twenty-three mortar fuses, fifteen cluster bomb units, fifteen homemade claymore mines, two protective masks, a typewriter, a chicom field radio, two demolition kits, a Soviet Flag, and twenty pounds of maps and documents.

The documents captured indicated that elements of the 1st and 3rd Battalions of the 274th VC Regiment had moved into the area in preparation for the "68" Tet Offensive."

The intelligence reported by Master Sergeant Nelson's team resulted in the destruction of two VC Battalions without the loss of a single American soldier.

Nelson saw to it that the men were completely professional while on missions but would allow them to blow off steam and relax in the base camp. It was a challenge to keep the men gainfully occupied between missions. To help with morale, the first sergeant allowed cookouts, beer parties, and rough and tumble games of "combat football" where he was knocked around just as much as his men.

As the long range patrol became operational, a need developed for additional personnel. One of the men had broken both ankles while going through Recondo School. He was patrol point man and was to have been first out of the helicopter. The tall grass made the LZ look deceptively close and he jumped out as the aircraft descended, still some 30 feet in the air. Replacements were also needed for Miles and Coonrod, so a recruiting effort was organize. Representatives from the unit would put on their camouflaged "tiger" fatigues, black berets, and visit the 9th Division Replacement Center in search of volunteers.

The replacement center was where the division's new arrivals could acclimate to the tropical climate. They also received classes on such subjects as enemy tactics, detection of booby traps and the importance of respecting the South Vietnamese people and their customs. On March 15, 1967, two future patrol leaders would meet at the replacement center. Private Johnston Dunlop was a 32 year old enlistee from Auburn, New York. Hilan Jones' 26 was a draftee from Thermopolis, Wyoming. Being older than the average recruit, Jones and Dunlop spent a lot of time together at the repo depot and became best of friends. Both were highly intelligent and competitive. They were intrigued when just before departing for their respective units, soldiers wearing black berets gave a presentation on something called a long range patrol.

1st LT. Rick Stetson, Master Sergeant Roy Nelson, and Sergeant Bob Hernandez represented the long range patrol that day. The LRRP recruiters told the new arrivals that they took only the best of the volunteers. Rank could be obtained faster in the long range patrol, and they would wear the black beret. Most important, because they operated in the enemy's backyard, the chances of becoming a casualty in the long range patrol would be much less than if they served in a line outfit.

It wasn't long before Jones received word that he had been picked to become a LRRP, and was ordered back to Bearcat. He hitched a ride to the division's base camp on an armored personal carrier. On the way, he passed an engineer unit building a bridge. There covered in dust from head to toe was Dunlop. Jones yelled over to him "I'm going to be a LRRP." Dunlop shouted back, "me too." They would soon be reunited as members of the long range patrol and achieve notable success as patrol leaders.

In April, members of the long range patrol were sent to Nui Dat Phuoc to work with the Special Air Service (SAS) of the 1st Australian Task Force as part of Operation Port Sea. The LRRPs quickly took to working with the Aussies who were excellent fighters that appeared to be calm in battle. When contact was made with the enemy, the Aussies attacked with every bit of fire power at their disposal.

It was during Operation Port Sea that a patrol led by Sergeant Ray Hulin made the April 29, 1967 edition of the Army Reporter, in an article headlined," 9th Infantry Recon Team Forced to Kill Four VC." The patrol had been monitoring a trail when a group of enemy soldiers from the 5th Viet Cong Division passed by. "After the first enemy force passed, we waited ten minutes before the point man stepped out onto the trail to see if anyone else was coming," Hulin said. When the point man, SP4 James Elder, saw an enemy patrol ambling down the trail, he signaled Hulin. "He let me know we didn't have time to fade back into the jungle so we just squatted down and froze," Elder said.

Elder was behind a small bush only a foot or so off the trail while the rest of the patrol was position about ten meters further back. The first soldier passed without seeing the LRRPs. As Hulin reported afterwards, "He had his weapon on his shoulder and was looking at the ground. The second man stopped right in front of me. When he turned and faced me, it shocked him like he didn't know what to do." Sergeant Hulin knew what to do and unloaded a magazine of ammunition into the man. The other patrol members fired on the remaining Viet Cong. "I just kept shooting until I didn't see him anymore," said SP4 Fred Jenkins."

The team broke contact and moved back to set up a defensive position as the enemy fired away with an automatic weapon. Hulin called for extraction and as the team lifted out, gunships swept the area with machine gun and rocket fire. For his decisive action in leading the patrol out of danger, Ray Hulin received the Bronze Star and was promoted to Sergeant E-5. It was proof that rank could indeed be gained rapidly for those patrol members who were willing to assume the responsibility of providing sound leadership.

The long range patrol did not have its own table of organization and equipment (TO&E) so requisition could not be made through normal supply channels. There were shortages in equipment and weapons so the men had to scrounge the best they could by wheeling and dealing. 1st LT Garrison and staff sergeant Cottrell were two of the best when they first arrived in the D Troop area, the living conditions included few creature comforts. Garrison was determined to do something about the lack of electricity. He told SSG Cottrell to accompany him one day and they set off in a duce and a half for a headquarters compound near Saigon.

Generators seemed to be in abundant supply and many were being used to provide power to the living quarters of the numerous generals who were housed in the compound.

Garrison grabbed a clipboard and trying to look as official as possible, walked up to a warrant officer and said "I'm here to pick up my generator." As the warrant officer gave him a puzzled look, Garrison continued, "That generator over there is the one on my list to pick up," pointing to a high-powered model intended for one of the Generals.

"But I am not authorized to load any generators," protested the warrant officer. Garrison reached into the truck's cab and produced a bottle of Jack Daniels Whiskey. "Here," he said offering the bottle. "This might help convince you to load that generator on my truck." A wreaker was located, the generator loaded, and Garrison and Cottrell headed back to Bearcat with the new piece of equipment. The generator was well received by the members of D Troop and the LRRPs. The patrol members returned to Bearcat on April 17th after operating with the Australians. Shortly after, Ed Garrison accompanied a patrol and would observe while running as point man. The officers were turning over patrol leadership to the NCOs but still went out whenever possible as the young sergeants gained experience. As point man, Garrison was to be the first one out of the helicopter. As he sat with his feet on the Huey's skid he noticed the LZ had been prepped by artillery rounds that had stirred up clouds of dust. It appeared they were about to touch down so Garrison jumped out while the aircraft was still 3-5 feet in the air. He broke his foot when he hit the ground and was evacuated to Japan after spending the night in the jungle.

He was three-months recovering and would not return to the long range patrol. After his foot healed, he was assigned to Company C, 2nd/60th where he would excel as the executive officer. (XO) His battalion commander was so impressed with his performance as XO, that he went all the way to General Westmorland to receive permission for Garrison to command a Rifle Company.

Captain Tedrick transferred to a staff job at division headquarters and left the unit in April. That left 1st Lt Stetson as the remaining officer and he commanded the unit from April 3- 30, 1967.

Then 1ST LT. Donald Lawrence transferred from an infantry company to join the LRRPs. Stetson and Lawrence had graduated together from OCS Class 1-66 at Fort Benning and had the same date of rank. Their class had graduated alphabetically and since Lawrence had walked across the stage before Stetson it was decide that he would command the unit.

One of Stetson's patrols was known as "the great elephant hunt." Reports had come into headquarters that numerous elephant tracks had been spotted in the division's area of operations. The G-2 wanted a patrol to investigate and determine if the VC were using the elephants as beast of burden to transport food, weapons and ammunition. The members of the patrol were Rick Stetson, John Berg, Steve Ross, Marlin Mears, and Hilan Jones. The insertion took place without incident. As the patrol moved out the next day, it was not long before the unmistakable signs of elephant tracks were visible in the thick bamboo. The patrol followed the wandering tracks, but did not find any elephants.

They moved into their evening position and later that night, the patrol members heard the trumpeting sound of the elephants calling one another from distance parts of the jungle. The next night, the patrol set up not far from the embankment of an abandoned railroad. They monitored the site but there was no sign of enemy activity. Sometime after midnight, the patrol was jolted by the sound of automatic weapons being fired from the other side of the rail embankment. It sounded like at least a platoon's worth of weapons being fired on full automatic, seemly right next to the startled patrol. The firing continued for at least a half a minute and then ended as suddenly as it had started. There was complete silence. No voices, no sounds of magazines being removed, just a "thump, thump," as each patrol member heard the sound of his pounding heart. The men remained on high alert until the normal sounds of the night convinced them that the VC must have been conducting a test fire of their weapons and moved on. The patrol was extracted the next day without finding the elephants.

Not long after that patrol, however, Stetson was in a Huey providing command and control for an insertion when he happen to look out the door of the aircraft as they returned to base camp. Standing by some trees, at the edge of a small clearing, was a mother elephant and her calf. He pointed them out to the pilots who banked the helicopter for a better look and more elephants were observed. There was no sign of enemy personnel, just wild elephants, annoyed at the sound of the circling helicopter, running and trying to hide in the trees. The Pilots sent a message to the other D Troop aircraft that they had elephants in sight. In no time a transmission came from division headquarters wanting to know the status of the elephants. It was then announced that the commanding general was boarding his helicopter to come out and take a look for himself. As the D Troop helicopters flew back to the airfield, called the Roundtable, a growing group of VIP's were seen circling the area looking for the elephants.

Elephants were not the only animals the patrols had to contend with in the jungle. Stetson was on a patrol one day in thick jungle when an object of some kind crashed through the leaves and landed nearby. The patrol members instantly froze with fingers on the triggers of their weapons while minds raced trying to determine what had been thrown at them. Was it possible a VC had tossed a dud grenade at them? Was someone trying to lead the patrol into an ambush? After waiting several minutes, no further sounds were heard and the patrol cautiously moved forward. "Thump," another unknown object landed close by. The men did not move as they kept their weapons pointed to the front, sides, and rear of the patrol. This time Stetson decided to remain in place until the source of the noise could be located. Again the rustling of leaves. They looked up and saw a group of monkeys, swinging through the branches while staring down at them. The men breathed sighs of relief while shaking silent fists at the monkeys who were either defending their territory or amusing themselves by seeing who could hit a soldier with a stick.

The 9th Infantry Division established a base camp in the Mekong Delta called Dong Tam. The 600 acre base camp on the My Tho River was formed by dredging sand from the river bottom and depositing it on the marshland. The world's largest dredge was used to perform that task until Viet Cong sappers planted explosive charges on the dredge one night sending it to the bottom of the river. Smaller dredgers were used and the division soon had a permanent base in the Delta.

The division needed intelligence about enemy activity in the area and long range patrol members were flown to Dong Tam to meet with the Navy SEALs. The SEALs were an elite and secretive group that had established a reputation for successful operations in the swampy Delta region. The SEALs were known for specializing in prisoner snatches where they would stand in water up to their noses for hours waiting for the opportunity to grab a high-ranking prisoner. During January 1968, the Navy SEALs and LRRPs began joint operations. The missions designated as SEAL-ECHO were highly selective patrols. They were inserted by Navy patrol boats, helicopters, and Boston Whalers.

The 9th Division placed units of the 2nd Brigade on board the USS Benewah (APB-35) the flagship of river Assault Flotilla One. The Benewah, a converted WW 11-era LST, was first launched in 1946. It was modernized in July 1966. Included was a helicopter landing platform and accommodations for 1150 soldiers. The feature that made the biggest impression on the patrol members who visited the ship was that the troops slept in air condition quarters.

An instructor at the MACV Recondo School had told his students that a patrol leader always had the final approval for a mission. It was pointed out that if a patrol leader had been given an assignment that he considered too dangerous, he had the option of turning down the mission. When the assignment came down from division for the long range patrol to put a team in the Delta, a young sergeant was given the mission. He was taken on an over flight of the area and quickly observed that instead of lush jungle offering concealment the instant a patrol moved off the LZ, the Delta was nothing but wide open rice paddies. When the helicopter landed, the patrol leader said he would have to refuse the mission, as it was too dangerous. Stetson, the operations officer, knew it was pointless to try to force him to take the patrol as the sergeant's apprehension could endanger the entire group. Stetson said he would lead the patrol and put in an immediate request to have the sergeant transferred out of the unit.

The patrol was deposited in the middle of a rice paddy at last available light. Instead of scrambling for the thickest clump of vegetation, as they would do in the jungle, the patrol tried to conceal themselves as best they could behind a two foot high rice paddy dike. They lay motionless hearts pounding, imaging that every VC in the area knew exactly where they were. After a period of time had passed, the stillness of the night reassured the patrol they had not been spotted. The men were still uncomfortable at being so exposed but eventually they relaxed enough to resume normal breathing. The patrol was not far from a small river and sounds of motorizes sampans could be heard moving throughout the night. Early the next morning, the patrol was picked up. They did not have a lot of intelligence to report but they had demonstrated it was possible to spend at least one night out in the open. Patrols operating in the area would later learn how to use the vegetation along the riverbanks for concealment and would go on to accomplish numerous successful missions in the Delta.

The network of rivers and canals around Dong Tam offered another means of inserting patrols; by boat. Thoi San Island was in the middle of the My Tho River and was a favorite location for the VC to fire at passing patrol boats. The enemy was so prevalent the soldiers called the place VC Island. On May 9, 1967 the LRRP's received a mission to put a recon patrol on Thoi San Island. They would be inserted at last light by a Navy armored troop carrier that was armed with a .50 caliber machine gun, two 20mm cannons and several deck mounted caliber .30 machine guns. SGT Ray Hulin was to lead the patrol. Also on board was Stetson the operations officer, a reaction team lead by SSG Cottrell, that included Howard Munn, Bob Hernandez, First Sergeant Roy Nelson, Dennis Marable, one other LRRP and a five man Navy crew.

Stetson peered through the growing darkness trying to locate a suitable spot to insert the patrol. The first site selected was not a good one. As the boat eased into the island, it was apparent that the water was too deep and the bank undercut giving the men no foothold when they would scramble ashore. The boat backed off and moved further down the island. A small clearing was spotted that had a gradually sloping bank and Stetson gestured for the sailor at the wheel to head the boat in. The troop carrier had a landing ramp in front but it was decided that dropping it would expose everyone in the boat to hostile fire. The patrol members crouched along the ledge that ran around the top of the craft, ready to drop over the side as soon as the boat got close enough to the island. The sides of the boat were covered with bar armor; long thin rods about six inches apart that helped prevent RPG rounds from penetrating the hull. The rods served as excellent hand and foot holds as the team members climbed over the side.

The point man was the first to leave the boat and wade into the waist-deep water followed by Hulin the patrol leader. The third team member was climbing down the side of the boat when one of the men still on the ledge whispered "I hear voices," At that moment, automatic weapons opened up from the shoreline. Bullets pinged off the hull as the boat's operator threw the engines into reverse backing the craft towards the middle of the river, while another sailor returned fire with the .50 caliber machine gun. As the reaction team sprayed the riverbank with their M16's SGT Cottrell manned the .30 caliber machine gun. Stetson took a quick head count and realized they were a man short. He glanced down over the side of the boat and he spotted Hulin fighting to hold on to the bar armor. As patrol leader, he carried a heavy radio plus his weapon and all his equipment and he was unable to hold any longer, as they rapidly backed out into the river's current, SGT Munn, who was splattered in the arm by fragments from a bullet was manning one of the .30 caliber machine guns when he spotted Hulin in the middle of the river, trying to shed his pack and web gear. Stetson shouted for the navy personnel to stop the engines as Munn executed a head first dive into the river and swam towards Hulin. As he approached, Hulin calmly turned his back so Munn could reach around and help keep him afloat. Just as he placed a hand on his chin, Hulin gulped in a mouthful of the muddy river water. The more the patrol leader shook his head trying to spit out the water, the harder Munn held on until the boat was finally able to maneuver, and pick up the LRRPs. Munn was recommended for the Soldiers Medal for his actions and in September 1967, he received a Bronze Star with V device for his heroism.

Insertion by boat was the exception as most patrols were dropped off in LZs by helicopters flown by the skilled D Troop pilots. A close bond of mutual respect developed between the aviators and the members of the long range patrol. The LRRPs knew if a patrol experienced trouble, the pilots of D Troop would do whatever necessary to get them out. The aviators and members of the long range patrol not only worked together; they were friends so that when a tragic accident occurred on May 26, 1967 both units were devastated. The gunship crews (Crusaders) often operated at night. Sometimes they would support American or South Vietnamese units or they might go off in pairs trying to stir up targets on their own. The D Troop pilots were highly capable of night operations. New pilots were arriving in country on a regular basis and before sending them out on missions, they would train on orientation rides to become familiar with combat flying. On May 26, CPT Norman Kidd and 1st LT. Jack Dodson reported to the D troop operations area for briefings. Both had been in Vietnam only four days and would be flying as observers with two veteran gunship crews that night.

The new pilots were attentive during the briefings and tried to absorb as much information as possible about the tactics of gunship operations. The D Troop pilots, having conducted such operations numerous times, were relaxed and eager to show the new arrivals how the gunship's firepower could be unleashed on an enemy who liked to move at night.

When Stetson reported to night operation the next day to plan a mission, he could immediately see by the pilot's faces that something was wrong. There was none of the bantering and carrying on that usually took place in the building. Instead, one word, "midair," summed- up what happen. Two D Troop gunships had been conducting night operations outside a small Vietnamese town when the aircraft collided in flight. One of the door gunners survived the impact but died shortly after being airlifted to a hospital. The rest of the pilots and crew died immediately in the crash. The Doughboys rifle platoon was flown in to help secure the crash site and help with the removal of the bodies. Killed in the collision, were Captain Gene Matthews, Captain Robert Mosher, Warrant Officer Robert Cook, and Specialist Five George Bennett, Specialist Four Rodger Fortune, Specialist Four Joseph Le Grand, Specialist Four Melvin Martz along with the two aviators that just arrived in country, Captain Kidd and 1st LT Dodson. Their deaths cast a dark show over the men of D Troop and the long range patrol.

SSG Richard Cottrell, a 36 year old patrol leader from Philadelphia, received an operations order on June 23, 1967 to conduct a long range patrol reconnaissance patrol in Long Thanh Province south of Bearcat. His team consisted of Sp4 Dennis Marble, who was the assistant team leader, PFC Marlin Mears, James Woodson and Hilan Jones. The insertion was scheduled to take place the following afternoon.

There was a good amount of experience on the patrol. SSG Cottrell was a graduate of the MACV Recondo School and had completed 12 successful missions. SP4 Marble was honor graduate of his Recondo class. PFCs Mears and Woodson were also Recondo school graduates who had accompanied Cottrell on several missions. PFC Jones was the "new guy" and had received a letter of completion from the Recondo School.

As the team prepared for the mission by drawing rations, filling canteens, cleaning and test firing their weapons, Cottrell took an over flight to help select the landing zone (LZ) for the insertion. Preparations completed, the team headed for the Round Table late in the afternoon to board a waiting Huey for the insertion. The patrol members had the usual nervous tension that took place just before each mission but this day, the anticipation was even higher as the "new guy" had not been tested in combat.

Adrenaline was rushing and hearts pounding as the helicopter neared the LZ. The heat rushing in the open doors and the "whop, whop, whop," sound of the blades changed pitch while the aircraft flared for a landing told them they were moments away from scrambling into the jungle. The patrol dashed for the nearest concealment and froze in place as the sounds of the choppers faded away. This was a crucial moment! Senses trained to pick-up any sight or sound made by the enemy, who might have been watching the LZ. If they had been spotted, this is when the VC would start looking for them. Minutes passed and the quiet of the jungle became reassuring. Finally, the operations officer circling high above in the command and control ship asked on the radio how the light was. "Red" meant trouble and "green" indicated everything was good so far. The light was green so the gun ships, the pickup aircraft, and the C&C ship headed back to Bearcat leaving the patrol on their own. The men moved into the jungle in search of a suitable night position. Cottrell selected a spot in the thickest undergrowth they could find and the patrol settled in for the night. The experienced men rested well but Jones was more apprehensive and got little sleep.

The next morning, the patrol moved out on their pre-planned route and came upon a well-used trail. It was early in the day and footprints were visible in the mud. It was obvious the trail had been used recently and the enemy had to be nearby. Cottrell decided to take up positions and monitor the trail. He moved his men across and placed them in positions about five meters apart where they paralleled the trail and could observe without being detected. It wasn't long before the first enemy soldier was spotted moving quickly along the trail, coming from the right of the patrol. He was wearing an olive green uniform and carrying a chicom rifle, holding it by the barrel as it rested over his shoulder. Following about 20 meters behind came another similarly dressed and armed solider. Behind him came another and yet another NVA soldier.

After waiting several minutes and seeing no additional enemy, Cottrell moved the patrol briskly away from the trail and out of the area. The patrol had traveled just a short distance when they came upon a small clearing where they found a poncho shelter erected on four bamboo poles stuck in the ground. Under the shelter was a five gallon square can with the top cut off. The area looked as if it had been occupied recently and Cottrell assumed it was an outpost for a larger complex nearby, probably located in the direction where the enemy soldiers had come from. Sensing there could be an ambush in the vicinity, Cottrell directed his point man, Jones to head off at a ninety-degree angle away from the outpost and a possible ambush. As they were moving away from the clearing, the patrol members heard a rifle shot and a muffled explosion that sounded like a grenade. The team immediately went into the standard reaction drill used to break contact, escape and evade (E&E). Each LRRP assumed a position with every other man facing to the right or left. The last in line; Marble, faced the direction of the enemy and fired his weapon on full automatic. He emptied his magazine and turned away to run from the enemy reloading his weapon as he ran. Each man would in turn repeat the procedure before following the assistant team leader.

Jones, the last to fire, emptied his magazine and tossed a white phosphorous (Willie peter) grenade before turning to catch up with the escaping team. As Jones tried to run through the thick vegetation, his rucksack became entangled in the "wait-a-minute vines." He quickly shed the pack and left it on the ground as he caught up with the patrol. They ran for several hundred meters before stopping to listen and determine if they were being followed. They were not and the patrol leader called for an extraction. Afterwards, Cottrell was quoted in a newspaper account of the action as saying, "We hit our firing plan and moved out smartly." The Old Reliable paper continued the dramatic account: "It gets hairy out there" Cottrell said frankly, "That business was a surprise and we don't like to get surprised. It was good thing we used our diversionary tactics, it was a close shave." Cottrell and Marble received the Bronze Star with V device for the actions on the patrol while Jones was awarded the Army Commendation Medal with" V" for valor.

The long range patrol received considerable publicity for a June 1967 patrol led by SSgt Robert Syndram. The old reliable June 24th edition headed the story detailing the patrols action as, "Five Man Recon Team Bailed out of Tight Spot by Arty and Gunships." The Stars and Stripes carried the same story under the heading, "9th Inf." Recon Team's Ordeal. The VC were 10 to 1 against us. Out Numbered 10 to 1, a five man team from the US Army's 9th Inf. Div. Long Range Reconnaissance Patrol became the pray of a Viet Cong manhunt recently. After five hours of fight and flight, the team escaped the enemy thanks to the pinpoint accuracy of artillery fire and a withering onslaught from helicopter gunships.

A lone enemy soldier had spotted the recon team. SP4 Donald Naughton of Norwalk, Ca. was forced to mow down the approaching enemy with his M16 rifle. The chattering gun gave away the team's position. "They knew we were in there and they were determined to find us," team leader SSG Robert Syndram of Ft Wayne, In. recalled afterward. The team attempted to avoid detection by moving frequently but twice narrowly missed being mowed down by enemy machine gun fire. Breaking for a nearby knoll and surrounded it as the team desperately radioed for aid. After three hours without making radio contact, the 9th Division artillery observer's plane arrived overhead for a routine radio check.

The surrounded troops explained the situation to 1st LT. Stewart McGregor, the aerial observer. McGregor radioed artillerymen at the Black Horse base of the 11th Armored Cavalry Regiment, about three miles west of the knoll at about 2:30 PM the first rounds thundered in on the enemy position. "They were good; close groups and right on target," the observer recalled. "The rounds were coming in right on their heads," Syndram remarked.

Meanwhile, helicopter gunships of the 9th Division's D Troop, 3rd Squadron, 5th Armored Cavalry, had scrambled. The artillery fell silent shortly after 3:30 PM and "that's when the gunships took over," McGregor related. Rockets and mini-guns raked the enemy position to secure a landing zone where another chopper from D Troop could land to pick up the team. CPT. William (Wild Bill) Bailey and WO William Brayshaw landed the rescue chopper about 200 meters west of the knoll. The team sprinted to the waiting helicopter. At 4:30, five and half-hours after the enemy force had first surrounded them the recon team was on its way back to the division's base camp.

There was serious anticipation by the LRRPs as Captain Clarence "Clancy" Matsuda arrived and took command. Matsuda, a 30 year old "Seasoned Veteran," had successfully commanded A Company, 3rd Battalion, 60th Infantry and was awarded the Silver Star for his actions at Ap Bae. He was handpicked to take over the LRRPs, charged to "straighten them out," and instill some much needed professionalism as well as discipline. Matsuda's strongest attribute was leading by example. One of the first policies established by the captain was that everyone going on patrol would apply camouflage paint to their hands and face. This basic principal in reconnaissance was often overlooked by a number of LRRPs, making it an ideal place to start in creating the self-discipline and professional attitude necessary in this type of unit.

By July 1967, the 9th Division's long Range Patrol platoon had been operating in Vietnam for almost half a year. During that time, the LRRP's had obtained valuable intelligence about the enemy within the division's area of operation but just being a platoon size, the number of patrols that could operate at any given time was limited. Thus, the decision was made by the 9th Division to increase the LRRP Detachment to a company size unit.

The unit was given priority to be filled at the 100% level utilizing volunteers who would be screened through an interview process. When it came to selecting his officers, the new commander took advantage of his West Point Connections. One of his good friends at the Academy, MAJ Jim Blesse, was the 9th Division assistant G-1 and in charge of assignments for company grade officers. He let Matsuda have his choice of all incoming lieutenants and as a result, hard charging young officers Dale Dickey and Henry Richard Hester were assigned to the rapidly expanding unit.

LT Edison K Woodie did not join the LRRPs through the replacement pipeline. He served with Matsuda in the 3rd Battalion, 60th infantry as the Heavy Mortar platoon leader. Woodie was a Ranger qualified officer with an outstanding reputation as a strong (he had been a body builder competitor) and courage's warrior. Matsuda "arranged" Woodie's assignment to the LRRP's through Major Blesse. Like Matsuda and the other hand picked officers, Woodie led by example and was eager to get in the jungle and start patrolling. Woodie's sense of humor fit in nicely with the LRRPs who never minded pulling the legs of non-rangers. One time a soldier asked Woodie why his survival mirror had a hole in it. (The mirrors were carried by all patrol members and the opening was to help aim the mirror at an aircraft.) With a straight face Woodie said to the soldier "that's so if I am shaving while in the field, I can look through the mirror to make sure no Viet Cong are sneaking up on me."

As Matsuda's officers began putting plans into effect to build the unit into a company, the new commander left Bearcat for an orientation tour to observe how other units were utilizing their long range patrol assets. His visits would take him to the 173rd Airborne Brigade, 4th Infantry Division, 1st Cavalry Division, 101st Airborne Division, 196th Light Infantry Brigade, and the recon Battalion of the Fleet Marine Division. In addition, Matsuda stopped in at the MACV Recondo School where he obtained lesson plans and operating procedures that would become useful when his units developed its own Recondo training program.

Returning to Bearcat with a better understanding of the organization and direction he wanted for his unit, Matsuda summarized the observations during his visits as follows: 1.) The support of the LRRP's varied according to the confidence their senior leadership had in the unit, and, 2.) LRRP's must believe that they belong to an elite unit made up of tough fighters. The warrior spirit had to be part of the temperament for those selected to perform commando operations in Vietnam.

To help instill the "Warrior Spirit," one of the first requirements the new commander implemented was that patrols members would be fully camouflaged before going out on a mission. This meant applying green and black "grease paint" to all areas of exposed skin to include ears and the backs of the hands. Prior to Matsuda assuming command, patrol members would smear little camouflage on their faces, but it was applied in a haphazard manner with thought that darkness would engulf the patrol after they were inserted and that the paint would quickly wash off in the rain and humidity. Matsuda, however, likened the application of camouflage before a mission to American Indians applying war paint to their bodies before going into battle. The process of darkening their skin by using camouflage sticks served notice that the patrol members were preparing to be sent onto hostile territory. In a previous assignment as a recon platoon leader, Matsuda noticed that the soldiers who put on the most camouflage always seemed to perform better. The LRRP commander wanted his soldiers to have every possible advantage over the enemy.

Matsuda made a point of taking an active role in his new company. Soon after taking command, he selected a team already scheduled for a patrol, and joined as an observer. The team consisted of a relatively new Team Leader, Sergeant Jimmy Bedgood, and Assistant Team Leader, Sergeant Kenneth McCarns. The three observers were Specialists Four Jerry Wilson and Hilan Jones, with Private First Class Bruce Church, filling out the team. Matsuda's role was to observe, hopping to get a feel for what type of "animal" he had been charged with shaping up.

There was nothing special about this particular patrol. Just the average LRRP team on a normal recon mission; searching for enemy locations or activity. As the team prepared for the mission, Bedgood made the over flight and selected the Landing Zone. Once this was accomplished he returned to bearcat for the remainder of the team. There was plenty of excitement among the patrol members as it wasn't an everyday thing to have an officer, especially the company commander, on patrol with them. Each man wanted to do his very best to impress the captain, not yet knowing that this mission would call for exceptional effort to just get out alive.

The insertion and first night out was uneventful. Things were going well as each man wanted to show his stuff for the commander. Camouflage sticks were used and the guys moved with extra care, to demonstrate for the captain they knew how it was done. The second day out began as the first had ended, uneventful. They had moved a thousand meters or so, without incident, when one of the men saw signs of fresh digging off to the right. Bedgood moved his team closer to inspect the area and attempt to identify what, if any enemy activity was going on.

They found a large circular hole about ten feet in diameter, dug straight down approximately fifty feet. Straddling the hole was a pole six to eight inches in diameter supported on two similar poles, about five feet tall, secured firmly in the ground on either side of the hole. Indications were this apparatus was being used to hoist the fresh diggings from the hole. The team moved back away from the digging and took a position where they could observe the hole without being detected. When the scheduled air relay passed overhead Bedgood reported the findings and requested support to provide security and investigate the hole. The team waited for any special instructions. No support was immediately available and the nearest LZ was a thousand meters away. It was decided that they mark their location and observe the area the remainder of the afternoon and through the night.

To get an exact location of the hole, Bedgood requested a "fix". This was a procedure used to determine a patrols location by flying over their position on the ground. Guided by the Team Leader or radio operator, the pilot of the approaching aircraft is given direction using the clock method (i.e. fly 2 o'clock) until he passes directly overhead. At that time, the radio operator would announce touchdown. The pilot would than fly in from a different direction and the procedure was repeated. The pilot then had an X on his map, marking the location on the ground and providing the co-ordinance of the requested "fix". Their precise location would prove to be become very important the following day.

The patrol spent the night alternating who would sleep and who would watch. They anticipated enemy soldiers or workers to come and continue the digging. This did not happen and the patrol moved out early the next morning. Having traveled a very short distance, they came upon a well-used trail with more fresh digging on either side. Under construction was what appeared to be fighting holes or bunkers? There was an eerie feeling among the patrol members as if "Charlie" wasn't too far away.

Bedgood took Jones and proceeded to move down the trail to their right. The remainder of the guys stayed in place providing rear security. The two hadn't gotten more than a few meters down the trail when they heard voices. It was unmistakably "Charlie" but he wasn't visible through the thick underbrush. Without a word, Bedgood lay down in the middle of the trail and opened up on full automatic in the direction of the voices. Calling for Jones to follow him, he turned and headed back at a double time to join the others. Before following, Jones emptied his magazine and tossed a couple of grenades up the trail hoping to discourage the VC from following. It didn't work and the patrol could hear movement and talking as the enemy made their way towards them.

The LRRPs went into their immediate action drill in an attempt to separate themselves from the enemy pursuit. Each of the six LRRPs fired a full magazine on automatic and the last man tossed another grenade as they ran away from the contact area. Having ran for over 600 meters they came to a small mound of dirt where the team leader decided to stop and listen for anyone that might be following. They set up in a small circle with McCarn and Matsuda watching the rear, Bedgood and Church to either side, with Jones and Wilson looking in the direction of their travel. It appeared that no one was following so Wilson and Jones decided to have a smoke before they moved on.

Before they had a chance to light their smokes McCarn opened fire on full automatic. He and Matsuda saw two or three VC picking their way carefully through the jungle looking for sign of the LRRPs. As the enemy fell, the team was up and running again, putting as much distance as they could between themselves and the enemy. They quickly covered another 600 meters or so before they slowed to listen for the enemy. It looked like no one was following. Breathing a sigh of relief, they continued toward the LZ for extraction.

As the team traveled quietly through the jungle they came upon a poncho covered structure of some sort. Jones always carried a few extra grenades and he saw this as an opportunity to toss one. The team took cover as Jones tossed the grenade toward the structure. The explosion shook the surrounding vegetation and Jones as well. He was hit on the head by a small fragment from the grenade. Further investigation revealed a rice cache, which the LRRPs destroyed before moving on to the LZ.

Reaching the LZ, they waited for the chopper that was on the way to pick them up. It wasn't long before the chopper was within radio range and Bedgood was directing them to the LZ. As the chopper came in to pick them up the pilot realized the area was too small for landing. As the chopper lifted upward, the pilot informed Bedgood of a suitable opening about 1000 meters from their present location. Anxious to get out of the area the team quickly made their way to the opening identified by the pilot. The LRRPs, with the help of the door gunner pulling and their teammates pushing, were able to load the chopper and lift off without any further problems.

Prior to going on a patrol, care was also taken to subdue anything that could reflect light, such as a knife handle, by covering it with olive drab duct tape. In addition anything that might rattle, such as rifle sling holders, was taped down. Tape even covered the openings to the barrels of their weapons, not for noise and light discipline, but to keep out mud and debris that might cause a rifle to jam as well as to help keep out moisture from the ever present rain. The midst of enemy contact was not the time to discover that a rifle would not fire, so patrol members would test their weapons prior to departing on each mission.

As the long range patrol expanded to a company, it was obvious that a larger living area would have to be found. The arrangement of housing soldiers with D Troop worked well when the LRRPs operated as a platoon-size unit and that allowed for strong bonds of friendship to be formed with the helicopter pilots and their crews. Now however, space would be needed for living quarters, an orderly room, operations room, classroom building and supply room as well as sufficient area to construct an obstacle course.

Division gave the unit a piece of property near the northern edge of the base camp and the LRRPs were ready to begin construction on their new home. Most of the work would have to be done by members of the unit as the Army engineers were stretched thin by combat missions such as operating Rome plows to widen roads through the surrounding jungle. The Engineers did agree to pour cement foundation for the buildings and fortunately the long range patrol had experienced carpenters such as Richard Cottrell, Elbert Walden, Greg Nizialek and Herbert Vaughan. To help handle the construction, soldiers without carpentry background received some quick OJT (on the job training) and were soon up on roofs driving nails alongside the more experienced hands. The men even handled the installation of the wiring needed to bring power to the buildings. One well-meaning patrol member who said he knew something about electrical work apparently got his wires crossed and was thrown from a ladder as he worked on a hot line leading to one of the buildings. Fortunately, the only thing injured was his pride.

LT Woodie was tasked with building the obstacle course. He rounded up "volunteers" to assist with lifting the heavy logs to be anchored in place for the rope climbs and other obstacles on the course would prove to be a highlight whenever VIP's would visit the LRRP compound. Tyrone Muse and Astor Pagan were two of the fastest and most agile of the group and were designated as the primary demonstrators. Visiting dignitaries would look on in amazement, as Muse and Pagan would scramble up a vertical wall and then almost free fall their way down the other side, slapping at the boards as they descended.

The quarters constructed in the new compound were nicer than those offered to soldiers in a rifle company. The officers and senior NCO's had individual rooms in their buildings and the soldiers were allocated space for their bunks and gear. Matsuda believed his LRRPs deserved the best. After spending anywhere from three to five nights sleeping on the ground, eating cold meals and communicating by either hand signals or whispers, the commander wanted his men to have a comfortable place to call their own when they came in out of the jungle.

Matsuda's designs for the company area required considerable more construction material than the engineers had allocated. The large classroom buildings, based on a similar facility he had seen while visiting the MACV Recondo School, would by itself require large amounts of plywood and roofing tin. Plans were also drawn up for an operations building, with space for situation maps, a communications room and a separate area for debriefings after missions were completed. In D Troop the patrols were debriefed in the soldiers sleeping area. The commander wanted the new facilities to be as professional in appearance as the men who would live and work in them. It was apparent the new accommodations would be a lot larger than the plans authorized, but Matsuda's philosophy was, "It is easier to ask for forgiveness than to ask for permission."

To obtain the massive amount of material needed for all the extras planned for the company area, including a separate building for their own club, the LRRPs resorted to scrounging, an age old Army tradition at which the patrol members were quite proficient. Lt Lawrence was tasked with heading up the "gathering patrols." Utilizing good recon techniques, he located an engineer storage area stocked with piles of roofing beams, plywood, tin, and other needed construction materials. Lawrence obtained a deuce and a half, designated one of the patrol members as his driver and proceeded to the unguarded storage area to see what was there to be appropriated. He discovered that the construction materials were bound together in large stacks and much too heavy to be lifted on the truck. The LRRP officer found a young private operating a forklift and asked the soldier if he would be interested in receiving a genuine set of tiger fatigues, just like the ones worn by members of the long range patrol. Lawrence told the soldier all he had to do was use his forklift to place some bundles of plywood in the back of the truck and the fatigues were his. The forklift operator said he would be happy to assist in the loading.

Because a forklift was not available back at the construction area, unloading the truck called for some ingenuity. Sgt. Emory Parish devised a solution that was not "by the book" yet managed to get the building materials offloaded in a fast and efficient manner. *As* Parish drove his overloaded truck into the LRRP compound with tires and sides bulging, he looked for a place where he could unload his cargo. The duce and a half was not built to be a dump truck but Parish made it act like one by revving the engine while popping the clutch causing the front end of the truck to rise up and letting the cargo slide out the back and land in a cloud of dust next to the building under construction.

Cement was another material that was hard to obtain. The engineers had allocated enough to pour the foundations of the living quarters and orderly room but providing additional cement for buildings like an NCO club was out of the question. The LRRPs however, were always up to the challenge of obtaining materials that were in short supply and hard to find. Patrol members discovered cement was being mixed at a plant outside Bearcat and trucked through the main gate by soldiers who might be interested in a set of long range patrol tiger fatigues. All they had to do was to divert their loads to the long range patrol company area and pour cement into forms that were already set up in the shape of an NCO club. The LRRPs supply of tiger fatigues went down a bit but they got the foundations to build their buildings.

Masonite was a material in short supply yet it was just what the LRRPs needed to finish the interior of their club. Always on the alert for an opportunity to meet their supply needs, the men noticed that a chapel under construction happened to have a supply of Masonite stacked nearby. In the belief their club was more in need of a finished interior than the chapel, a truck was dispatched under the cover of darkness and a load of the scarce material was transported back to the LRRP compound where it was nailed into place on the walls of the club. When the carpenters building the chapel showed up and discovered their Masonite was missing, the post chaplain launched an investigation that somehow pointed him in the direction of the long range patrol construction site.

It was an unhappy chaplain who visited the long range patrol compound and asked for the unit's commander. Clancy Matsuda was not in the area at the time so the chaplain turned to the highest ranking LRRP he could find, First Sergeant Roy Nelson. The chaplain, a Lieutenant Colonel, demanded to be taken on a tour of the buildings. Upon entering the club and spotting his Masonite, the chaplain locked Nelsons heel's (stood him at attention) and in a very un-chaplain like tone of voice, told the first sergeant that since the material was already nailed in place inside the building he would allow it to remain there if Nelson would guarantee there would be LRRPs in a attendance at future services. And so it happened that for a number of Sundays thereafter, members of the long range patrol "Got Religion" as they set together in the front pew of the base camps newly-constructed chapel.

Building operations flourished as a steady stream of hard-to-obtain wood came rolling into the LRRP compound on a regular basis. The unauthorized method of requisition continued under the direction of LT Lawrence until one day he asked a gathering of his fellow officers why he had to be the one who always took chances with the procurement. LT. Stetson said that since he did not have any patrols going out that day, he would be willing to lead a resupply mission. After Lawrence gave him the particulars, Stetson rounded up Emory Parrish to be his driver and they set off for the engineer supply area for a load of plywood. A forklift operator was located who accepted his set of tiger fatigues and quickly went to work loading the truck with bundles of the precious wood. Stetson was watching the truck grow heavy with plywood when he noticed a jeep slow down and an officer in the passenger seat view the scene in wide eyed amazement before speeding off. Shortly thereafter, a jeep with two large letters on the hood, "MP," pulled into the area and two soldiers wearing armbands with similar letters, approached Stetson and asked who had authorized him to load materials from the engineer's storage area. The lieutenant replied that he had no such authorization but that since there were no signs identifying the areas being off limits, he had assumed the materials were there for whoever needed them. One of the MPs said, "Sir," you will need to come with us and your sergeant needs to unload that truck."

Stetson, with visions of his days as an officer coming to an end, was escorted to the MP headquarters where he was interviewed, and a statement taken. The MP Commander said he would release the lieutenant if Captain Matsuda would write a letter of reprimand to be placed in Stetson's permanent records. The letter was written and a copy sent to the MP's but Matsuda somehow "misplaced" the original that was intended for Stetson's file and no further action was taken.

Fortunately, the construction phase of the new long range patrol area was nearing completion when Stetson got "busted" but his apprehension by the MP's prompted a visit from a major on the staff of the Division engineers who had been instructed to determine how much material the LRRPs might have appropriated over the previous months. It did not take a math genius to compute that considerably more material had been used in the construction than had been authorized but by that time, the wood had been cut and nailed securely in place. The major, while unhappy that so much material had been stolen from the engineer's storage yard, did seem to appreciate the fine quality of construction by the long range patrol carpenters and he allowed the wood to remain in place.

When it was completed, the LRRP's spacious new living quarters, operations and classroom buildings equaled anything to be found in

Vietnam. Their own club provided a boost to morale and was a favorite place for patrol members to unwind when arriving back at the base camp after a mission. Matsuda appointed Non Commissioned Officers to manage the bar on a rotating shifts and a Vietnamese day laborer named Lon was paid to clean the club after parties held the night before. The lively parties would often include guest such as helicopter crewmen from D Troop and music blaring from tape decks, the gatherings would last late into the night. The company commander would try to have the men lower the volume, oftentimes without success, and the first sergeant usually let the music play on as he understood the need to let his men relax and blow off steam.

The LRRPs prevailed upon the Special Services to provide a pool table for their club and the men obtained a black and white television. The Armed Forces Network aired only one channel and programs such as "The Tonight Show" was several weeks old by the time they reached Vietnam. The news, however, was current and was read by soldiers from a studio from Saigon. There was considerable interest when war broke out between Israel and Egypt and shows about past wars were also popular. Roy Nelson remembers the time his men loaded into a helicopter made its way back to the base camp, Stephen Noomen pulled the tape back from Nelsons watch and yelled into the first sergeant's ear, "Hey Top, we'll get back in time to watch "Combat on TV."

The new compound adjoined the 9th Division's Old Reliable Academy which proved to be an advantage to the long range patrol. Not only did the academy have a mess hall which allowed the patrol members to eat their meals without having to perform the tedious detail of KP, but it also was where soldiers arriving in the division received an orientation prior to reporting to their units. The long range patrol was given permission to make recruiting presentations to the academy and the representation made a sharp appearance wearing their black berets and pressed tiger fatigues with LRRP scrolls on the left sleeves just above the 9th Division patch. The team members explained to the recent in-country arrivals that the LRRPs were not for everyone and only the most dedicated and physically fit would make it and be allowed the privilege of wearing the black beret. They went on to state that the excitement of operating undetected behind enemy lines in "Charlie's backyard" could not be equaled.

The only drawback to being next to the Old Reliable Academy was a bit of jealousy that developed from some of the academy's cadre who did not care for the "Hot shot" LRRPs who made recruiting trips into their area. Sometimes, especially after a few beers in the evening, words would be exchanged between the neighboring soldiers. To prevent any unauthorized hand-to-hand combat and to keep out uninvited visitors, Matsuda had concertina wire placed between the long range patrol and the Old Reliable Academy. As soon as the wire was strung, peace prevailed between the two units.

The LRRP's established a reputation as a valuable intelligence asset for the 9th Division. Even when a patrol came back and reported no signs of recent enemy activity, the information was useful to the division's intelligence staff and operations planners. It took a special soldier who would volunteer to conduct patrols deep in enemy territory and out of the range of friendly fire support. The missions called for courage, resourcefulness, integrity and teamwork. Most of the soldiers possessed the requirements to belong to an elite unit, but not all, and occasionally someone would find their way into the long range patrol that did not belong there.

LT Stetson had concerns about one of the sergeants who served as a patrol leader, an individual who did not seem to always demonstrate the qualities needed for a leadership position. On one occasion when Stetson was leading a patrol, the sergeant was assigned radio relay duty. As the aircraft moved close to the patrols position at the designated time, the patrol leader made contact with the sergeant, gave his report and asked for the location of the nearest LZ in case an emergency extraction was needed. There was a long pause and finally the sergeant came back and said he was unable to provide the information because "The big picture just flew out the window." Stetson realized that the sergeant's map had blown out of the helicopter and he imagined what would happen if it fell into enemy hands complete with reference points, frequencies and call signs. The patrol leader did not feel comfortable until the patrol was safely extracted.

The loss of the map was an accident so the sergeant was given the benefit of the doubt, and allowed to remain with the unit. In fact, it appeared he might have the makings of a dependable patrol leader when on his next mission; he managed to bring his men safely home after receiving enemy fire. The sergeant requested an emergency extraction after his patrol had made contact, gunships and a pickup aircraft were scrambled and the men were pulled out. When the patrol returned to Bearcat the sergeant said it had been a close call and as proof, pointed to his canteen that had a bullet hole through it. Reporters picked up on the story and the Old Reliable newspaper published a photo of the sergeant holding his canteen. The cut line below the photo said the long range patrol leader would be looking for a new canteen as "the one he is holding won't hold water". The caption continued "During a recent patrol the team leader spotted an enemy soldier 50 meters behind him. The enemy fired his rifle but struck the canteen instead of the sergeant."

Not long after the story was published in the paper, one of the men on the patrol came to Stetson with a troubled look and asked to speak with the officer. When asked what was wrong, the LRRP replied, Sir," that mission we were on did not happen exactly the way the sergeant said it happen." Stetson both anticipated and dreaded the response when he asked the patrol member if there had been any enemy contact, "No Sir," the soldier replied," Our patrol leader took off his gear and fired a round into his canteen so we would have a reason to get extracted."

With a knot forming in his stomach Stetson though about the pilots. The LRRPs had spent nine months in country developing a bond of trust with some of the Army's best aviators who would risk both aircraft and crew to pull a patrol out of danger even if the call came in the middle of the night. If that bond of trust was broken, if there was doubt in the minds of the aviators when they received a call for an emergency extraction, the relationship between the two units would be jeopardized. To prevent that from happening, the sergeant had to be removed from the unit immediately. No disciplinary action was taken because an Article 15 would slow down the out processing. Losing the privilege of wearing the black beret and the prospect of being sent to a line unit would serve as the punishment. Fortunately, the personnel office understood the need for the LRRPs to have trustworthy soldiers in the unit and in this rare instance when someone did not measure up there was no delay in cutting orders to remove him.

Training was a continuous process for the members of the long range patrol and some of their activities could not escape notice by soldiers stationed at Bearcat. For example, whenever the LRRPs trained on the McGuire rig which was nothing more than a long rope with a harness on the end so it could be dropped into the jungle when an emergency extraction was called for. In such a situation, the patrol members could slip into the McGuire harness and be pulled up through the trees to the helicopter hovering above. Roy Nelson was supervising one of the training sessions while wearing a foot cast from a previous injury. The cast however did not prevent Nelson from demonstrating how the McGuire rig worked and after snapping on the harness, the first sergeant was yanked into the air and took off high above the dusty base camp. At the same time, the commanding general emerged from his headquarters, looked up and noticed a soldier being pulled by a helicopter while dangling at the end of a rope while wearing a gleaming white cast on one of his feet. The general ordered his aid to find the name of the soldier who was going through that type of training wearing a cast, but Nelson never heard any repercussions. Perhaps when the general learned it was a LRRP first sergeant at the end of the rope, it explained everything.

Rappelling was conducted on a regular basis. There were not a lot of trees on the base camp but fortunately the D troop area had one that was suitable for rappelling training. The LRRPs constructed a platform about 30 feet off the ground, nailed some climbing boards on the trunk, and they were in business. Once the soldiers had mastered the basics of rappelling off the platform, they progressed to coming out of a hovering helicopter.

Physical training by the long range patrol was another activity that attracted attention. It was hard to miss a platoon of soldiers' double timing over the Bearcat streets while singing, "I want to be an Airborne Ranger, jump from planes and live in danger." Few of the units on the base conducted such activity yet the LRRPs realized fitness was essential in order for them to patrol with heavy packs and if the occasion demanded it, to outrun the enemy. Not all the men enjoyed running the base camp during the middle of the day in high heat and humidity, but the runs helped build conditioning, mental toughness and a sense of unit esprit as soldiers trying to relax in the shade would shake their heads and mutter, "There go those crazy LRRPs." Of course the runners would rub it in a bit by shouting, "on the right, sick call: sick call."

Word got out that when it came to training, the 9th Division's Long Range Patrol had things squared away. When the MACV Recondo School suspended operations in order to conduct training for their own personnel, arrangements were made for new in-country arrivals from the 101st Airborne Long Range Patrol to be trained by the veteran LRRPs from the 9th Division. Roy Nelson conducted the initial briefing for a lieutenant and his men from the "Screaming Eagles" division shortly after they arrived at Bearcat to begin their training. Nelson received the impression that because the lieutenant and his men were "Airborne," and he and his trainers were "legs, (non-airborne) there was not much need to go through training with the 9th Division soldiers. The 101st soldiers were not particularly attentive when Nelson said although most of the training would take place close to the perimeter of the base camp, there was still a chance of enemy contact and the same noise and light discipline procedures would be followed as if they were far from friendly support. In addition, he stressed the need for safety since everyone would be carrying live rounds.

The first sergeant's safety apparently did not reach all the airborne soldiers because as SP4 Daniel Salvadore helped teach a fast reaction drill just outside the berm at Bearcat, one of the new arrivals put a round through his leg. Nelson was furious when heard of the shooting, yet the airborne lieutenant acted as if it was, "No big deal" since Salvadore had "only been wounded." The first sergeant assured him that it was a big deal because one of his best soldiers had been taken out of action. He informed the lieutenant that he needed to round up his men and prepare to report back to his outfit.

Before the 101st soldiers left Bearcat they went on one final training mission and it too, did not go well. The training exercise took place near a rubber plantation where some of the airborne soldiers opened fire and killed a woodcutter and his water buffalo. Roy Barley was on stand down back at Bearcat and was asked to take his team out to the area in a duce and a half and load up the woodcutter's ox cart. They reached the scene but as Barley and his men struggled to lift the heavy wooden ox cart into the truck, warning shots were heard in the surrounding woods. The men left and headed to the woodcutter's village where his widow was paid for the loss of his life. Barley was surprised to find the woman received more for the loss of the water buffalo than she did for her husband. By the time they left the village it was dark so the men hurried back to the base camp. When he arrived, Barley asked about the soldiers from the 101st and was told they had packed their bags and left.

The 9th Division LRRPs continued to demonstrate they could find the enemy as indicated in an October 23, 1967 Old Reliable newspaper article with the headline, "LRRPs count 9 Dead VC after Brief Firefight," The article's dateline is "Long Thanh" and in it, Sergeant Hilan Jones was quoted as saying, "Our patrol was nearing a landing zone where we were to be extracted, when we noticed movement in a window of a hooch to our front." Jones, from Thermopolis, Wyoming, continued." As we crouched in the thick brush watching the hooch we could hear men talking about 50 meters to our front." Team member SP 4 Ed Beckly of Middletown, Conn. added. "About that time two men entered the hooch carrying weapons." The patrol leader then radioed for permission to move in the hooch." "I called for them to come out and when they heard me; I saw them ran for their weapons, recalled Jones, "So I threw a grenade in and we opened fire."

The firefight resulted in six enemy KIA and after sweeping the area before their extraction, the patrol detained a suspect found hiding in the bushes. In addition, four pounds of documents and six rifles were collected during the sweep. Jones and Beckly returned to the area with a reaction force from D troop about an hour after the patrol was extracted. When fire was received from a hooch in the area, the reaction force opened up resulting in one enemy KIA. During the sweep by D Troop, two additional bodies were discovered, two suspects detained and two small arms, 50 pounds of military equipment and 500 pounds of rice captured. There were no friendly casualties during the operation.

The same patrol was described a bit more dramatically by A.F. Gonzalez and A. Bryan in an Article titled "Flop Hat Jungle Rats" in August, 1968 issue of Saga Magazine. It had been a stinking mission. Here, the floppy-hatted GI scouts were dozens of miles deep into Viet Cong Territory and their Cambodian guide was puking his guts out, too weak to continue the clock-and digger patrol. Its leader, 26 year old Sgt. Hilan Jones, finally muttered, "Screw it," to himself and got on the radio to call in a chopper to get the team the hell out of there. They had been humping it out in the boonies for three days and hadn't seen a single Charlie.

The five men moved silently down toward the landing zone when suddenly Jones' hand went up for silence. From a hooch along the trail came the sing-song sound of male Vietnamese voices. Charlie was having lunch, mistakenly thinking he was safe and sound and a long way from Yankee firepower. The patrol fanned out and closed in, knowing they would have to get rid of the VC before the choppers came into ground fire range. The voices stopped as the Yanks tightened the noose. Jones crept toward the hut's back door, kicked it open, hosed down the luncheon scene with a whole magazine of M-16 ammunition and flipped in a grenade. As he hunkered down, a savage explosion tore the hooch apart and the Charlie's scampered through the hut's front door for safety. The other G.I.'s M-16 opened up and savage streams of fire crowed the doorway with the twisting bodies of dying VC. Six men were chopped down in a welter of blood. Two dove into the woods and got away. Another pair, blood soaked, quivered with terror, came out with their hands up, just as the chopper arrived and began to hover for the pick-up. A VC squad had ceased to exist in just 30 seconds.

We surprised them so completely," says Jones, "they never even got off a round at us. Out of the six rifles we captured, three chicom pieces and three American M-2 carbines, only one had a round in the chamber. It was more an accident than anything else. We weren't actually looking for that sort of thing."

In the "Saga" account of Jones' patrol. Reference was made to a "Cambodian guide." The 9th Division LRRPs started experimenting with the use of native guides during the second half of 1967. "These guides used to be ARVN scouts and for a time, a number of mercenaries from border tribes, (Cambodians for the most part) were assigned to the LRRPs. "We had our ups and downs with them" said Matsuda of the mercenaries." We had 12 of them assigned to us and four of them were real good. The rest sort of ruined the program for the good ones. Their endurance is very short and after three days humping in the field, they're just about shot. Some of them had problems with noise discipline. Surprisingly, we had a few that just couldn't control themselves once they saw Charlie in the field. They panicked. So rather than jeopardize the team, some of the team leaders refused to take the mercenaries out. Of the four good ones, I would say their sense and perception is better than ours. They pick up trails, signs; things we very seldom pick-up."

The LRRPs discontinued using mercenaries and instead, started, successfully working with VC defectors called, Tiger Scouts or Kit Carson Scouts. The defectors were usually familiar with the AO and as Matsuda pointed out; "They know the terrain, and they know how Charlie sets up traps; where to look for them and where to look for caches."

In November, a patrol's close call encounter with the enemy again made Old Reliable headlines in an article titled, "LRRPs slip away from VC dragnet." When the patrol, led by SSG Emory Parrish of Fullerton, California, first moved into their night position, they heard a single rifle shot and then nothing more than normal jungle sounds. After a couple of hours, PFC Thomas Perzanowski of Syracuse, Indiana began hearing increased jungle noises and sticks popping. "Noises seemed to be coming from my left, then my right and then to my rear."

The LRRPs remained silent until the intruders began throwing sticks in their direction, trying to get us to give away our position," according to Perzanowski. One of the sticks hit a bush in front of Perzanowski and then struck him. "The sticks were coming in from both sides, "he explained. The patrol leader used a night vision device and spotted two VC. One of them was carrying a chicom carbine,

Parrish added, "They were just standing around eyeing our area like they weren't sure we were there."

As the VC tightened their net, Parrish radio in a sit-rep and moments later, two helicopter gunships and an extraction helicopter were on the way. Then a VC who had advanced dangerously close to the LRRP position stepped on a stick which cracked loudly. The recon team quickly opened fire. "We maintained a steady volume of fire," stated Perzanowski. "On about my 15th shot, I hit a VC to my front."

The shooting continued for about 15 minutes at an estimated seven to ten enemy soldiers before the patrol broke contact and moved to the extraction LZ, each man grasping the belt of the man in front as they moved through the darkness. The patrol was safely picked up and Parrish was quoted afterwards, "None of our men got excited. Everyone functioned just as he was taught. If they hadn't, we never would have escaped that area."

Matsuda understood the stress produced by his men operating "up close and personal" with the enemy. So in addition to providing them with spacious living accommodations and a club in which they could relax after completing their patrols, the commander arranged for the LRRPs to receive two out of country R&R's, whereas most soldiers were allocated just one. He also saw to it that his men had priority when they made their R&R selections, so that most were able to visit the country of their choice. Movies were a popular way to relax between missions and there was convenient viewing next door at the headquarters company where a sheet tied to a wooden frame served as the screen while the audience set outside.

Through the ages, military units had pets as mascots and the long range patrol was no exception. A number of Vietnamese dogs found their way onto Bearcat looking for handouts and one: a white, medium-sized mutt with a black circle around one eye, wound up spending his time with the long range patrol. He was quickly adopted and named "LRRP" by the men.

LRRP was loved by the soldiers and he appeared in a great number of photos and slides. Never camera shy, it was almost as if he enjoyed posing. He was included in all activities and even took rides in a helicopter. Once Stetson rode in the back of a Huey to pick up a patrol, he took LRRP along with him. As the patrol members scrambled on board the hovering chopper, broad smiles broke out as they spotted their favorite dog. "LRRP," they said while giving him a friendly pat on the head. Unfortunately, the story of "LRRP," the long range patrol dog, did not have a happy ending as he was run over by a deuce and a half in Dong Tam. His memory, however, will remain with the soldiers who knew him for they considered the dog to be the long range patrol's best friend.

Just as soldiers reported to the 9th Division went through the Old Reliable Academy before beginning operations in the field with their units, those selected to become members of the long range patrol would undergo an intense period of training in the unit's own Recondo School before they could join a team. Applicants had already been screened prior to joining the LRRPs. Captain Matsuda required a GT score of at least 100, which was above average, because the men had to be able to read a map, plus have the ability to assume leadership of a patrol should the occasion demand it. There was also the interview process which would attempt to weed out those who did not possess the temperament required to be a LRRP. It took an individual who enjoyed the challenge of infiltrating into enemy territory, remaining calm as bad guys passed a stone's throw away, and someone able to endure the hardships presented by sleeping on the ground during rainstorms with no cover or protection against the ever-present mosquitoes and leeches other than the insect repellant they carried.

It took stamina to endure the hardship of spending nights in the jungle with little sleep or at best restless sleep. The slightest unfamiliar noise would have the patrol immediately awake with senses straining to determine if danger was present. If a soldier was to snore or talk in his sleep, one of the other patrol members would place a hand over his mouth while shaking him awake. The frequent downpours in the middle of the night made sleep difficult. Emory Parrish summed it up nicely in the "Flop Hat Jungle Rats" article when he said, "Out in the jungle the weather changes drastically. It's real hot during the day and at night it's freezing. Around one in the morning the temperature in the jungle may drop suddenly by as much as 15 degrees, from 75 down to 60. You're sweating all day- your clothes are all wet. Then at night it turns cold. You really feel it."

The applicant had to be a team player, able to follow orders given by the patrol leader and carry out his assigned responsibilities within the patrol. The men depend on each other for survival and there could be no weak links. Finally, those desiring to become a LRRP had to be in good excellent hearing and vision. Once a soldier had passed the screening process, he was ready to attend the 9th infantry Division's Long Range Patrol Recondo School and began the training required to become a LRRP.

While patrol members put the finishing touches on the classroom building and obstacle course to be used by students going through the Recondo School, the unit commander worked to produce a program of instruction (POI) that would detail every aspect of the training. The POI ended as a 19 page document.

The 9th Division Recondo School Program of instruction is a two week course to train Personnel in the specialized skills and techniques of reconnaissance: This program of instruction was derived from the varied experience of the 9th Division LRRP Teams operating in the Republic of Vietnam from January 1967 until October1967. Lessons learned from other LRRP units and the 5th Special Forces have been incorporated into this program of instruction.

The program of instruction broke the two week school into 12 major subject areas totaling 205 hours as follows:

Subject	Hours
Administration	3
Communication	7
Physical training	18
Medical Training	3
Intelligence	5
Patrolling	56
Air Operations	5

Weapons	13
Map Reading	23
Combat Operations	57
Critique/ Review/ Exam	7

Each subject was detailed in a separate annex that specified the number of classes, the length and the material that would be covered, for example, the 5-hour intelligence block of instruction was divided into three classes: VC Weapons and Tactics (2 hours), Terrain Analysis (2 hours) and Combat Intelligence (1 hour). The annex also gave a: scope for each class. The scope for terrain analysis stated: Teaches the student how to use a map and aerial photos and make a detailed overlay of likely VC routes, base areas and positions."

The physical training portion of the Recondo School included a swimming test (must be able to swim 80 meters). A PT test (sit-ups, pushups, pull ups, rope climb and one mile run). Confidence course (must negotiate a 30' high log walk, climb and decent a 40' vertical rope ladder with equipment, traverse a three log belly buster and a 20' rope commando craw). In addition, there would be daily road marches with full equipment, starting at two miles and concluding on the seventh day with a seven mile march that had to be completed in less than 90 minutes. Students would begin each session of physical training with repetition of Army drill. "Starting position; move, at my command exercise."

The largest portion of the formal instruction was devoted to patrolling. Classes included camouflage and concealment, escape and evasion, equipment and security, methods of infiltration and exfiltration, patrol preparation and survival. Patrolling also included five hours of immediate action drills where students were taught how to beak contact when enemy was encountered from the front, rear, or either side along with the principles of escape and evasion to be used if normal exfiltration was not possible. The students were broken down into five man teams with each team running two live fire exercises. The live fire exercise included use of the M-16 rifle, fragmentation grenades and white phosphorous (Willie-Peter) grenades. Live fire was also used in a patrolling class called "jungle lanes." The scope for this two hour block of instruction stated formal instruction in quick fire techniques and engaging camouflaged targets. Each student is accompanied by an instructor in quick fire techniques and engaging camouflaged targets. Each student is accompanied by an instructor and is walked through a jungle lane set up with pop up targets in dense vegetation. The student must find and engage the target quickly and effectively.

Students had to pass a two part final exam (map-reading and general subjects) with minimum grade of 70 before they could graduate from the Recondo School, but the real test if they would make it as a LRRP was the 57 hour phase called "Combat Operation." It began with a warning order for a patrol mission and as detailed in the program of instruction, the class requires the student to go through the entire process in the conduct of a successful reconnaissance operation. The students remain in the field approximately 2 days on an actual mission. Every recon team has a faculty advisor who evaluates the student on all phases of their performance.

The training patrols were inserted into what was considered a "cold" area of operation, one in which there had been little enemy activity in recent months. There were no signs posted telling the enemy to "Keep Out, "patrol training area." If Charlie knew there was a patrol with four "newbies" getting their feet wet for the first time, he might well come looking for such an inviting target. The training patrols at the MACV Recondo School in Na Trang also tried to insert into relatively cold AO's but the enemy was unpredictable and sometimes contact would be made and casualties taken. The student knew the mission was for real and hearts pounded a bit faster as camouflage was applied, weapons were test fired and the patrol moved out for the first insertion.

When the Recondo students had passed their written test, the physical test and the combat operation, they were ready for a graduation ceremony where they received congratulatory remarks from the LRRP commander along with a coveted black beret distinguishing them as a member of the long range patrol. Even though they wore a beret and a long range patrol scroll on their sleeve, Matsuda knew the true test of whether the soldier could cut it as a LRRP would come only after their first contact had been made with the enemy. He saw some return from a close call "jumpy and shaky" and did not want to go out again. If that was the case, there would be no ridicule, or no name calling, the soldier would simply be transferred out of the unit.

Patrols operated in the field under guidelines developed by Captain Matsuda in the unit's Standard Operations procedure (SOP). The 31 page SOP outlined all aspects of patrol operations and ten annexes dealing with such areas as infiltration and exfiltration methods, air operations; patrol organization and security, patrol equipment, fire support and reporting.

The organization and security annex listed the responsibilities and duties for each member of a five man patrol as follows:

A.) Point man- The first man in the order of march is the point man. He is responsible for frontal security, locating booby traps and immediate danger areas. He must maintain and follow an accurate azimuth and initiates halts in immediate danger.

B.) Team Leader-- He uses his discretion as to his position in movement. Usually, the most advantageous position for controlling movement is second in file. He ensures every team member knows his location at all times, guides the point man as necessary, notes distances covered, carries radio and makes radio checks, keeps an accurate and up-to-date patrol log. He must make an over flight of the area of operation, an inspection of all weapons and equipment, and rehearsal of all team actions and reactions. He carries a pill kit which contains:

    Codeine (Cough Suppressant)
    Destroampetimene (pep pill)
    Polymagma (Anti-Diarrhea)
    Tetracycline (Anti-Biotic)
    Darvon (Pain Reliever)
    Morphine Syrette (Severe Pain Reliever)

C.) Senior observer—He records distance and assigned flank security, carries the long antenna, and any other necessary equipment such as a claymore, etc.

D.) Senior observer-- He is responsible for assigned flank security, carries the spare battery for the PRC 25, and other equipment such as a claymore etc.

E.) Assistant team leader-- He is responsible for rear security, carries the URC 10 back up radio, erases the teams trail, keeps an additional patrol log and pace count, takes over as team leader if and when the team leader is wounded.

The SOP specified that each patrol member must know the nature and purpose of the mission including infiltration and extraction, landing zones, routes of travel, enemy and friendly situation, escape and evasion routes, supporting elements, call signs and signals and reporting times. "The SOP" also detailed the three formations used by patrols; file (used in movement), circle (long halts) and column (breaking contact and wide open areas.) The SOP contained the following procedure for breaking contact: "if the point man is compromised, he fires in the direction of the enemy until his magazine is empty. Simultaneously the team splits into a column, taking two steps to their respective flanks, the team leader moves to his right and the remainder of the team goes to the opposite flank of the man in front. As soon as the point man empties his magazine, he runs down the center of the column, and the team leader fires his magazine and breaks down the center following the point man. This procedure is followed to the 4th man in the column who throws a white phosphorous grenade, empties his magazine and breaks to the rear. The assistant team leader is the last man to fire. This procedure can be repeated until contact is broken, remembering that there is no lull between any of the magazines fired. The larger volume of fire and the "Willie-Peter" (grenade) is usually sufficient to break contact.

The mission of the long range patrol as stated in the SOP was "to acquire information about the enemy through visual ground reconnaissance." The paragraph following the unit's mission, was headed," Capabilities," and it contained a single sentence that reflected the commanders philosophy, one that would result in significant changes in the way the long range patrol conducted operations. The SOP stated the long range patrol had the capability to:

A.) To conduct visual ground reconnaissance in jungle type terrain for periods of 1 to 7 days.
B) To conduct small-sized ambushes on combat patrols.
C.) To conduct visual ground reconnaissance in the Mekong Delta for periods from 12 to 48 hours, unless the terrain permits extended operations.

Prior to Clancy Matsuda assuming command, ambush patrols were not considered. The LRRPs had been told they were reconnaissance experts and they should never reveal their location by making noise in enemy territory. With just five men on a patrol, it was thought too dangerous to open up on an enemy of unknown size. Matsuda, however, though of the LRRPs as "warriors," which meant that given the right opportunity, his patrol could take the fight to an unsuspecting enemy. Sound judgment would have to be used. It would be foolish to initiate contact on the point element for a VC company. Ambushes would have to be conducted in areas where patrols had radio contact so that if necessary, a reaction force could be dispatched immediately. The LRRP commander felt, however, that carefully selected ambushes would make the enemy apprehensive about operating in areas once considered safe and they were worth the risk.

Matsuda's addition of ambushes to the unit's capabilities did not win immediate acceptance by all members of the long range patrol. There were a few who pointed out there was no "A" in "LRRP." The commander knew there would be those opposed to the change and so the policy of sending out ambush patrols was implemented gradually. The majority of the patrols continued to be reconnaissance in nature but the patrol leaders knew that should the circumstances be favorable, an ambush could be conducted.

By November 1967, the final class of new patrol members was enrolled in the Division's Recondo School. When the 23 Recondo

The Early Years

students graduated on the 13th of the month, it would bring the long range patrol company up to 100% strength. Thus, Matsuda selected the date to be called "Organization Day." Not only would there be a graduation ceremony, but the unit would officially become E Company, 50th Infantry. To commemorate the occasion there would be a review of troops by the commanding general. Demonstrations of LRRP's in action and an open house to show off their new facilities.

The LRRPs worked hard in preparation for the big event. Buildings were cleaned, equipment displays were constructed, and coordination was made with pilots, rehearsals conducted for the demonstrations and practice runs were taken on the obstacle course. The company commander had the LRRP's Standard Operational Procedure and Recondo School Program of Instruction put in special binders and placed on a table in the entrance to the classroom building for visitors to look at. Stetson had concerns about the SOP being placed in the open as it contained sensitive information such as how patrols were inserted but CPT Matsuda assured his Lieutenant that only friendly eyes would be viewing their SOP. Instead of worrying about the SOP, the LRRP commander told Stetson he needed to prepare to serve as the commander of troops for the Parade formation. Matsuda explained that he would be with the commanding general in the reviewing party and that all Stetson had to do was to salute when the general stood before him and report, "Sir," Your long range patrol is ready for inspection."

Organization day finally arrived and the company area looked spotless and so did the men in their tiger fatigues, polished boots and black berets as they stood in formation at parade rest. Stetson in his best command voice, called the unit to attention as the commanding general approached. He gave a smart salute but when he looked at the two shinning silver stars on the general's hat, he suddenly lost his composure and shouted out, "Sir, your long range patrol is ready for instruction." The general gave him a puzzled look and Stetson quickly corrected himself saying, "I" mean, ready for inspection."

Despite the glitch by the commander of the troops, the commanding general was visibly pleased with the accomplishment of the division's long range patrol and their new facilities. In his remarks, the general praised the LRRPs for providing "a great deal of information about enemy movements, action and supply upon which larger units could act." After the general concluded his remarks, a demonstration of a LRRP insertion and extraction was held.

The following account of the Organization Day demonstration appeared in the November 29, 1967 edition of the Old Reliable newspaper: "A helicopter swooped down over LRRP headquarters, flared into a hover and dangled two 80' ropes earthward. In seconds, four heavily armed, camouflaged figures had rappelled to the ground and fanned out in practice formation. While a narrator explained the insertion procedure, a simulation contact was made and attention focused just outside the camp berm where a smoke bomb had been thrown. The smoke indicated the location of the LRRPs waiting for extraction while under enemy fire.

In seconds, a helicopter light fire team was making low level firing passes, spewing rockets and mini-gun fire. Additional passes brought the familiar whump, whump, whump of exploding grenades as the gunship's grenade launchers beat back the enemy in preparation for extraction.

The paper gave additional coverage in the December 6th edition when several photos were printed of Tyrone Muse demonstrating use of the confidence course. The cut-line read: PFC Tyrone Muse, 19 of Baltimore a member of the 9thDivision's LRRP detachment works out on the unit's confidence course during recent Organization day activities. In the top photo, Muse shows grim determination to pull himself across a tightrope bridge. Below, he leaps from a log bridge after sprinting across it."

December was a month of anticipation for the original LRRPs who had formed the unit at Fort Riley, Kansas for they were getting "short," which meant they did not have much time in country. All had been counting the days until their DEROS (date estimated returned from overseas) and they took pride in teasing the newer members just how short they were. (I'm so short I could fit in a matchbox!) There was also a sense of anticipation by all LRRPs because there was a rumor floating around Bearcat that the base camp would host a visit by Bob

Hope's traveling USO show. The famous entertainer had performed for some of their fathers during World War 11and every Christmas since he had visited overseas military bases during the Christmas Holidays. Many of the shows had been filmed for *TV* specials the soldiers had watched while growing up so they were fully aware of the huge boost to morale created when Hope showed up accompanied by beautiful singers, dancers, and actresses.

The itinerary for Hope's shows in Vietnam during December 1967 was classified. The Army did not want to advertise such an inviting target, with several thousand G. I.s gathered in front of an outdoor stage, ahead of time. However, when a stage was constructed at Bearcat it appeared what had been rumor might actually turn out to be true. The final proof came several days in advance when the LRRPs received word that Hope would indeed be visiting Bearcat but that headquarters wanted a patrol out in the jungle during the show to make sure there was no enemy activity in the area. Every LRRP had his heart set on seeing the Bob Hope Show, Ann Margaret was just one of the entertainers he had with him that year, and it was difficult selecting a team to pull duty while Bearcat watched the show. Finally, five men went out without incident and when the LRRPs returned back to the camp, they heard what a great performance they had missed.

At midnight on New Year's Eve, streams of red tracers filled the air over Bearcat as the Men celebrated the conclusion of 1967. It had been a year in which the 9th Division Long Ranger Patrol demonstrated it could operate in a hostile environment. One LRRP had been killed in action and a number had been injured or wounded. More would be lost in the years that followed, especially as operations picked up in the Delta and the LRRPs took the fight to the Viet Cong. The 9th Division LRRPs established a unit from scratch that went on to locate and help defeat a determined enemy up to the day the last troops were pulled out of Vietnam. The soldiers who wore the black berets in the 9th Infantry Division did their part towards contributing to the well-know and true motto: "Rangers Lead the Way."

CHRISTMAS 1967

BY

ROY BARLEY

I was all of 20 years old and not really looking forward to my first Christmas far from home, especially in Vietnam. I figured that the Bob Hope Christmas Show would be a great way to try to forget about home. Not so much for the show itself, but for all the other soldiers sharing the same fate and memories. The laughter was bound to help. I knew that as a new guy in the unit, having been there since Oct 1, 1967 there was a slight chance I might be called to run a mission during the Christmas truce but was reassured by my team leader James Martin that would not happen. Late morning of the 24th I was told to report to HQ. Along with myself were a number of guys who came in when I did, along with those who were in the Recondo School right after we were. I had been a team leader on the Recondo School mission and felt comfortable in the jungle running with Jim Martins teams.

    We were advised that we were selected (actually, the newest guys in the unit) to run missions to observe what the VC were up to during the truce. I remember the team I was on, consisted of some great soldiers, Jim Glaze (a two tour Veteran, Airborne and tough as nails), Greg Foreman (big blond surfer dude who I would latter run a number of missions with and who would soon have his own team), Bob Wallace, (quit and serious) and I forget who else was selected. I think that Wallace was the Team leader but I cannot be sure. The team was truly a throw together as we had never run missions together before, but since we all were trained and knew the SOP of the unit we felt comfortable. We drew our rations for 5 days and double checked our equipment as the selected Team Leaders did their over flight to select the LZs and see whatever they could see from the air. None of us were real happy about going out over Christmas but we all realized that it had to be done.

Christmas Eve we climbed aboard our birds that were to insert the various teams in the selected areas of operation (AO) at last light. There is a thing called pucker power. This is where your asshole shuts so fast that it glues your ass to the deck of the bird. This was what the level of tension the men were at as we prepared for insertion. All weapons loaded and ready, not knowing what was waiting upon landing. Actually landing was not quite what happened. Generally men left the aircraft between 10 and 4 feet, so all were on the ground in a matter of seconds as the bird swooped in and never really came to a hover. This and extraction were the most dangerous times of the mission. We had to find a place to hold up for the night and went further into the wood line. We crossed a hard packed wide trail and we were careful as we crossed it one at a time. It was getting dark and we found a bamboo thicket to hunker down in and not far off the trail (a couple of meters).

As darkness came quickly in the jungle the team had to quickly set up in a wagon wheel with all heads to the center. This was so we had 360 degree of coverage and that anyone trying to find us in the thick would make a racket trying to get to us. We had an over flight check sometime after darkness to make sure we were set for the night. I was too concerned with absorbing the jungle noise and listening for anomalies than to think about Christmas. I was the closest team member to the trail when we set up and I don't know how that happen, but if contact came from the trail I'd be first in line. After a while the tension kind of seeped away and my eyelids got heavy and I drifted off to sleep It was our standard procedure to sleep unless we had movement nearby. I know that sounds crazy now; 5 men, deep in enemy territory, falling asleep, but it always worked well. When I was going through the school it sounded nuts to me but it did work.

I don't know what time it was when I was awaken to the sound of oxen pulling a cart and the voices of the Vietnamese as they moved slowly down the trail that we had crossed a few hours before. The grunts of the oxen told me the carts were loaded with something that the VC would be using against us in the future. We had landed right next to a section of the Ho Chi Min trail. I silently prayed that they would just keep going and that my feet were in the bamboo thicket. At one point the convoy took a break and stopped to rest for a few minutes. The oxen train had seem to be endless as it moved along with noise; but when they stopped the silence was deafening.

At that moment one of the team members snored and before my hand could get to his mouth and nose several other hands were already there. The Vietnamese had heard the snore as excited voices sent one individual looking for the source. I did not even have my M-16 in my hands and moved quickly and silently to lay my hand on the handgrip and trigger while the VC decided to try to check out our bamboo thicket. He stopped right at my feet and was trying to see what had made the noise. I prayed that that no one would make a sound and that this VC would find nothing of interest and head back to his convoy. He stood there for what seemed to be hours as we fought every instinct to open fire, knowing that our orders were not to fire unless fired upon. Also knowing how dangerous a night extraction would be and we would not know what we were facing in enemy strength. I tried to silence my breathing as to not give him any reason to hang around. I could make out his outline and saw an AK at port arms. After a bit he spoke to his comrades and headed back to the convoy. I could hear them speaking before the convoy started up again, probably though it was a wild pig or some other animal. He never knew how close he came to dying that night and I was relieved that I did not have to take a life that night. As the convoy moving again with all its squeaks and groans and creaking of wood, Wallace moved his mouth to my ear and whispered: "If he comes back again put one round through his head and we head back to the LZ." I just did not have the heart to tell him that if he did come back again I would open up with all I had and hopefully make then think they had hit something larger than just 5 ordinary guys.

Needless to say we did not get any sleep the rest of the night as we listened to the ox cart convoy make its way down the trail. It seemed like hours before all movement stopped for good as the last ox cart went past. We had remained undetected and observed and listened to report what we had back to Division the next day. Christmas day started like any other day in the jungle of Vietnam ....hot and humid. While the team leader radioed the previous night's finding, I decided to see as much of the trail as I could from where I was. The trail had some wagon wheel ruts that it did not have the day before and you could see footprints right at the edge of the thicket. If the VC had taken one more step he would have stepped on me. Close!

The Team Leader told everyone that we were moving further from the trail as they wanted us to observe a trail along the trace. A trace was a path plowed through the jungle by large Roman plows that, it was hoped would stop movement of supplies by the enemy. This was obviously someone's idea that had never set foot on the ground. It was far from nice and neat as it looked from the air. Trees were down every which way and movement in the trace was very difficult for everyone. You had to climb over and under all sorts of mangled jungle vegetation that was laying all sorts of different ways. The VC had simply moved their trails to another sector of the jungle and went about business as usual. So on Christmas day, with whispered "Merry Christmas" to all and from all, we headed toward a new location. Actually it wasn't all that far (less than 100 meters) and located between the trace and the trail. It was a very small area to set up in. Somehow I ended up looking out on the trace, a ringside seat. There were some small trees amongst us and I had two fallen trees in between the trace and me. We ate some LRRP rations and observed the trace and the trail all day and into the night. We heard no more traffic on the trail and it was all quite that night and the next night also.

In the early hours on the 27th I had an eerie feeling that I was being watched. As dawn broke I had a visitor. There was an Ocelot at my feet standing on the log with its front feet and watching me. I had barely cracked an eye to see it and did not want to scare it away. I watched for as long as I could, about 5 minutes, and then I moved. It literally disappeared as it moved so fast. I kind of felt it was looking for a meal and was sizing me up. A very strange occurrence and not the last one I would have with the snakes and animals in the jungle of Vietnam.

The days went slow and the nights slower as we stayed in that one place much longer than we ever had before. I knew this was not good and against everything we knew about patrolling, but our job was to stay in place. The confirmation that we had stayed too long came on the 29th as I heard scratching on my poncho. When I lifted the poncho I had all sorts of nasty little things with pinchers trying to get to me. I think they were termites of some type but sure could bite. I decided to soak the area with bug juice and that got rid of them. The only problem was the smell given off of the repellent was foreign to the jungle and readily recognized by friend and foe alike. The poncho back in place seemed to kill most of the smell. At least those damn bugs no longer attacked me. We thought we were being taken out on the 29th (5th day). Imagine our surprise that we were to stay in place for another day. We had taken along rations and water for 5 days and were very low on both. In our AO there were no streams to refill from so we stretched what we had. On the 30th we again were told that we had to stay in place. And this was not good in that the trail became active again along with the far side of the trace. Not good.

The morning of the 31st we were told to stay in place. This time I got on the radio and told HQ that there would be no need to pull us out, but to send the body bags, with the graves registration team. We had over stayed our time and our luck was running out. We had no food or water at this point and were really running on pure luck.

It was around 1 pm when we were advised to prepare for extraction. We waited on the edge of the trace and soon as the bird was on its final descent, we headed toward it through all the entangled brush and fallen trees. The pilot had landed some distance from us and we had to hustle through that mess to get to the bird. It was not one of our regular pilots and this guy was a real ass-hole. We made it and were extracted with no incident. After we arrived at the company area we were debriefed. After a hot shower and a few beers we set around drinking as 1968 came around. The base camp opened up with tracers, etc. when midnight arrived. What a holiday it had been.

L to R Sgt Ken McCarn, SSGT Arylan Wieland,
and First SGT. Roy Nelson (1967)

Tyrone Muse (1967)

Sgt. Bob Hernandez (1967)

L to R Sgt. Ken McCarn, LT Hester, Capt. Clancy Matsuda,
Sgt. Mike Patrick, and Sgt Bob Hernandez (1967)

Capt. Clancy Matsuda in center with 9th Division Commanding General and staff (1967)

LRRP Roy Barley

L to R Lt Dale Dickey and SSGT Elbert Walden 1968

SGT Hilan Jones 1968

L to R Pat Lafferty, Gary Jones, David Stone, Rick Ehrler, Tony Hanlon, Nick Selby and Jim Martin 1968

Sgt Duane "Poncho" Alire 1968

Ready for another ambush 1969

Ranger Gerald Cody in the Mekong Delta

Sgt Bob Bryan and best friend Ranger Marshall Larsen

Ranger Ron "Tess" Tessensohn

Taken the day the unit became E Company 1967

Last photo taken of E Company Rangers in July 1970

KENNTH RAY LANCASTER "MIA"

BY

TONY HANLON

It had been almost a year since the first casualty, Leroy Lynn Miles, of the LRPD. Kenneth Ray Lancaster of Silver Spring, Maryland, became the second while in the final phase of training, on a combat patrol, at the MACV Recondo School. There are varying accounts of that fateful morning of 3 January, 1968. Following is the most accurate as seen through the eyes of a man that was on that mission, Tony "Ape" Hanlon.

"I feel I need to set the record straight concerning the events regarding Ken Lancaster's death. The excerpt from "Rangers At War LRRPs in Vietnam" is not true. There was no fire fight that morning. The following account of the events that day is as accurate as I can remember."

I had the misfortune of being with Ken Lancaster on the student patrol when he fell from the chopper skid. There were seven men on the team: Special Forces Sergeant First class Jason T. Woolworth, one Korean liaison officer, Lieutenant Chi Keen Hong, Kenneth Lancaster, George Kozach, William Ridge, Tony Hanlon, and a Korean student. We had inserted at dusk into a very small landing zone halfway up a mountain side. The chopper couldn't land forcing us to jump five to ten feet to the ground. As point man I was the first out, then Woodworth and Lancaster, followed by the remainder of the team. We grouped, set a perimeter, monitored the area for a bit, and then proceeded down the mountain. Near the base of the mountain we found a super high speed trail four to five feet wide. We crossed the trail, got to the bottom of the mountain and started up the other mountain. I don't remember how far or how long we traveled but we did take a break.

I need to regress too shortly after I arrived in the Nam. I cut one or two coils off the spring that held tension on the selector switch so I could flip my M-16 to auto easier and quicker. While moving in the dark, somehow my selector switch was moved to semi. During our rest stop I was moving slightly to adjust my position, my M-16 resting against my left shoulder, the barrel near my cheek when it discharged. After I got my vision back we were told to move out. We moved up the mountain for the remainder of the night. At daybreak we came upon a somewhat level area overgrown by elephant grass. The team prepared the pickup zone while SFC Woodworth called for extraction.

Now here's the really f—ked up part. Three birds came into view from behind the mountain, the pickup bird and two Cobras or Gunships, I don't remember for certain which. I do remember all three choppers were firing everything they had. The pick-up bird came in, set one skid near the ground and hovered while the team loaded on. To our amazement there were two men riding on the pickup bird. We scrambled onto the chopper and it lifted off unaware that Lancaster and Kozach hadn't gotten on board and Lancaster was holding on to the skid as we lifted off the ground. I don't remember how high we were when we became aware of Lancaster's grave situation. The team members on that side of the chopper tried to pull him in but were unable to. When Ken fell, it was as if time had stopped.

This was a f__king nightmare and shock. I need to back up to the extraction. We (the team) didn't know there were two pick up birds, the second one picked up Kozach without incident. Why were there two pick up birds? Who knows? I don't. SFC Woodworth was the most learned man on the team. He should have been the last one into the chopper. However, Ken Lancaster did what we were all about, making sure his team was safe, costing him his life. Rest in peace Ken.

"1968"

COMPILED BY

HILAN JONES

Kenneth Marze was drafted into the army and started infantry training at Fort Pork, Louisiana in July of 1967. If you have ever been to Louisiana in the middle of the summer, you can appreciate the miserable heat and humidity. About the only good thing to say about it is that you were acclimated to the conditions of South East Asia without having been there. This was a plus as most all of the trainees would be going to Vietnam upon completion of their training.

Marze was no exception and after a 30 day leave, he arrived at the Bien Hua Airfield in the Republic of Vietnam on January 5, 1968. Marze was an 18 year old, full of piss and vinegar, anxious to get the war over with. Stationed at the 9th Division base camp at Bearcat with the 2/47th infantry he learned that the LRRP's were looking for volunteers. He threw his name in the ring to become a LRRP and by the end of January 1968, he was accepted.

Marze was a husky lad and certainly looked the part in his camouflage battle dress, hands and face painted black and green to blend into the surrounding jungle. He was indoctrinated into the LRRP's fast and was selected to fill in on a ten-man ambush patrol. Preparing for his first mission, he was thankful for the training at Fort Polk, as the weather was hot and sultry.

The ambush was set along a trail that showed visual signs of recent use and gave a high probability of success. The patrol barely got the claymores in place and settled into position when 10 NVA came walking down the trail. The guy that was supposed to set off the claymore missed the signal so the patrol leader hollered out for him to detonate the ambush. The NVA were well into the kill zone when the ambush was initiated and in the excitement of battle Marze stood to get a better line of fire. The concussion (back blast) from the claymores threw him about 10 feet, slamming him to the ground. Stunned by the force he quickly got to his feet, thankful to be alive. On his cherry mission Marze helped to eliminate ten enemy soldiers, received his indoctrination onto the LRRP's and earned his Combat Infantryman Badge (CIB)

On January 24, 1968, near Binh Son, a Long Range Reconnaissance Patrol that included Team Leader Greg Foreman, observers Thomas Wayne Hodge, Edward Chaffin, George House, and Gary Hollenbeck, were moving cautiously along a trail. Indication of heavy and recent use was visible as they came to a crossroads. Foreman and House moved out to investigate the crossing, the other three stayed put to provide rear security. Chaffin saw four Viet Cong coming up behind Foreman and House preparing to fire on them. Acting quickly and decisively he, Hodge, and Hollenbeck took them under fire. There was an intense fire fight and Hodge was fatally wounded.

The VC was lucky this day as Hollenbeck and Chaffin's weapons jammed. Both men applied immediate action, clearing their weapons, as Foreman retrieved, the mortally wounded Hodge, they continued to pour heavy fire on the pursing enemy, breaking contact using the standard reaction drill. The team began their escape and evasion as the VC regrouped and started to pursue the LRRPs. With the enemy in pursuit it became necessary to leave Hodge. Team members covered his body with leaves, twigs, then booby trapped his body. The patrol continued their E&E (escape and evasion) arrived safely at the pickup zone, the team was extracted and returned to Bearcat. There they were met by a LRRP reaction force that returned to the scene and retrieved Hodge's body. Thomas Hodge was posthumously awarded the Silver Star in recognition of his action that was instrumental in allowing the team to inflict heavy casualties on the enemy and make it safely to the pickup zone. Chaffin and Hollenbeck would later be awarded the Bronze Star with V device for their action.

Only the best were called to be LRRPs, including the chain of command. Lieutenant Dickey received his tutelage while performing as one of the operations officers under the best commander at the company level in Vietnam, Captain Clarence Matsuda. Upon Matsuda's departure in February 1968, Lt Dickey took command and the LRRP Company never missed a beat. "There were no precedents for protracted operations in a water filled land five feet above sea level. The trackless, inundated wastes south of Saigon, required learning on the job as the VC were pursued. Their finest forays and contacts being history, the LRPD had gained a reputation among friend and foe alike. An elite, cohesive, determined, hard charging unit, they proudly carried the nick name of "Reliable Reconnaissance" into their second year of combat.

When the division base camp moved to Dong Tam, located in the Delta, an opportunity came for some of the LRRPs to cross train with the Navy SEALs. Marze was one of the first to go on a mission with a SEAL team. It was an experience he will never forget. Only if you have been there and smelted the stench of death could you ever imagine what it was like.

Most SEAL insertions were at night, dropping off navy patrol boats (PBR) and walking in to a predetermined objective. This particular night the SEAL team, with Marze as a member, was inserted and walked about six kilometers. They came to an area with several hoochs scattered in the Nipa palm. What the patrol thought to be a small village turned out to be a large NVA base camp. It was near 0100 hours when two SEALs opened the door to one of the hoochs and stepped in. The hooch was lined with cots on both sides, occupied by about 30 sleeping NVA. Marze was providing rear security as the two SEALs opened fire with their Stoners (an automatic weapon with 150 round drum). A young VC girl wounded two SEALs and the interpreter when she threw a grenade from the hooch as she tried to escape out the rear of the hooch, Marze shot and killed her.

As the patrol pulled out of the area, Marze picked up the wounded interpreter in a fireman's carry. The wounded SEALs were able to move on their own, as they waded and swam numerous canals making their way back toward the river. The surviving NVA were yelling and firing their weapons as they searched for the SEAL team.

The team made it to a rice paddy, about 1500 meters from the contact area, before they were pinned down by automatic weapons fire and occasional mortar fire. With the wounded men it was impossible to get back for extraction by boat so the team leader called for a helicopter pick up. Marze was later quoted as saying, "I never will forget while we were pinned down, I was laughing while this SEAL was crying."

The helicopter was sent at about 0230 in the morning to pick them up. The LZ was hot and initially the pilot refused to go in and make the pickup. The Navy Chief told him if he didn't come in, they would shoot him down. There was a short lull in the firing and the pilot came in to pick up the team. The chopper hovered just off the ground as the SEALs scrambled onto the chopper. The navy chief was the last one aboard and took a round that was fortunately stopped by the battery in the radio on his back. The chief submitted Marze for an award but the paperwork was lost and nothing came of it.

A team led by Staff Sergeant Johnston Dunlop spent some tense moments in Long Thah Province as the team observed the movement of about one hundred Viet Cong. It was late afternoon when the team entered the Binh Son Rubber Plantation about eight miles south of Bearcat. Within thirty minutes after the insertion the patrol spotted ten Viet Cong soldiers moving along a well-used trail. "As time passed, we continued to see uniformed enemy soldiers," related SSG Dunlop, of Auburn, New York. They were well armed with AK-47 rifles and 81 mm mortars. Over 100 enemy soldiers counted in the next couple of hours. At dusk, Dunlop called artillery on the trail as the enemy passed. "When the shells hit; the enemy would move off the trail. They would wait, and move on after the shelling stopped." After the patrol was extracted, SSG Dunlop flew over the area with an Air Force forward air controller and pinpointed the enemy location. Division artillery bombarded the location.

The VC used various ways of communicating and was forced to improvise due to a shortage of radio equipment. Some used single shots to communicate, sometimes they struck bamboo sticks together, and lanterns were sometimes used at night to communicate as well as navigate. Marze was to learn this on his second mission out, a five man reconnaissance patrol.

Normal insertions took place early in the morning or near last light. This seemed to be the times that contact was least likely to happen. Most times LT Stetson would be on the chopper used to put the LRRP team on the ground. He and the team leader would make sure the correct LZ was used. This day was no different than many before. It was an hour or so before dark and the Huey was flying at tree top level. A cobra gunship was providing support from near-by. The insertion chopper came upon the LZ and briefly touched down. The five LRRPs hit the ground running and moved into the tree line before the Huey was back in the air. The choppers would remain in the vicinity long enough for the team to get settled into their night position.

The team moved into to the jungle some 300 hundred meters and circled for the night. They had been on the ground for thirty minutes and all was quite. The team leader gave Stetson the all clear saying "the steak is cold," the LRRP code that meant that all was clear. If the "steak was hot," the team would be extracted for insertion into the alternate LZ. As the darkness engulfed the five men, all that could be heard was the "Fuck You Lizard," calling out fukuuu, fukuuu, fukuuu!

The following morning the team was up and moving early. Things were uneventful most of the day. After traveling a couple of thousand meters through thick jungle, stopping several times to listen for any sound of the enemy, at 1100 hours they stopped for "pot time." Pot time was 1100 to 1300 hours when the VC would stop for lunch and an afternoon rest. If you moved during this time you were at a disadvantage as the VC being stationary would be more apt to hear your movement.

Late in the afternoon the team started to look for a good place to spend the night. The vegetation thinned and they found themselves in a complex of trails. Before they could move out of the area there was VC on both sides. All they could do was lay low and wait for an opportunity to escape and evade. As darkness fell they could hear the VC knocking bamboo sticks hitting together signaling that the team was in the area.

Bonding of Warriors

Fortunately the patrol found some dense under growth and watched the entire night as lanterns glowed all around them. Thinking the patrol had moved out of the area, the VC gave up their search and moved on. The remainder of the patrol was uneventful and the team was extracted two days later. Once back at base camp there was time to relax, drink some beer, and swap stories before the next time out.

Prior to the Tet offensive there were several sightings of large groups of NVA and VC units moving to and from Saigon through the Binh Son Rubber Plantation. The LRRP commander put two LRRP teams together for a special ambush mission. On February 17, 1968, ten LRRPs were inserted into a landing zone just inside the plantation. One of the teams consisted of Staff Sergeants Hilan Jones and Elbert Walden, Sergeant Mike Rohr, along with Specialist Four Donald Dupont and Dave Long. The other team was made up with a group of team leaders, Specialist Four Tom Eggleton, Sergeant Ed Rasen, Staff Sergeant James Glaze, David Sellens, and a private who had just joined from the l0lst Airborne. The patrol was designed for the teams to work in concert while at the same time independently in the event that escape and evasion became necessary.

The LRRPs were inserted early that morning without incident. They moved quickly to stake out a major trail and set up the ambush. Jones and his team set up on the right, facing the trail. Eggelton set his team up on the left with about forty meters separating the two teams. Walden, Rohr, and Dupont provided security on the fight flank while Glaze, Sellens, and the l0lst guy secured the left. Eggelton and Rasen strung Claymore mines in their portion of the kill zone as Jones and Long set up on the other side.

Shortly after the wiring of the ten claymores was finished and the ambush was in place, three NVA soldiers came moving down the trail from the right to left of the patrol. The ambush was not quite set and they were allowed to pass. Soon to follow was the main force (in excess of 50 NVA soldiers) in full battle gear. The three that had passed earlier turned out to be the point element for the larger group. The NVA soldiers were moving quickly along the trail with only a meter or so between soldiers. Each had a weapon. One carried a mortar tube another carried an RPG rocket launcher. All carried rifles, with several carrying rocket grenades and mortar rounds. As the NVA passed into the kill zone Rasen blew the mines on the left and Jones followed blowing the right.

All hell broke loose as team one came under heavy automatic weapons fire from the trailing enemy that were not caught in the kill zone. Unaware that team one was engaged in a heavy fire fight. Rasen, Sellens, and Glaze ran out to search the kill zone and capture any NVA soldiers that might be alive. Eggelton and the other guy secured the left flank. In the confusion of the battle, the handset cord on Jones' radio was pulled off at the connection to the PRC25 radio. The remaining NVA broke contact and retreated back down the trail in the direction that they had come. Team one then engaged in securing the right flank and assisting in the search of the bodies on the trail. Specialist Long discovered an NVA soldier tossing a grenade in the direction of Sellens and Rasen. The grenade exploded and shrapnel hit Sellens and Rasen before Long could cover the NVA and take him prisoner.

The LRRPs completed the search of the kill zone which produced the capture of a wounded NVA soldier, an RPG7 rocket launcher with rocket, an 81MM mortar tube, several RPG rockets and mortar rounds, several small arms, plastic explosives, and several pounds of documents. Eggleton called for extraction as the teams completed their search and moved to the pickup zone.

It wasn't long before the choppers were on the scene with the first Huey on the ground making the pickup. Dave Long carried the wounded NVA to the chopper as Rasen, Sellens, Glaze, Dupont, Rohr, and the 101st guy filled the chopper. Four men left on the ground came under automatic weapons fire from the near-by wood line and Eggelton took a round through both legs.

Walden threw a white phosphorous grenade marking the wood line that the NVA were firing from, secured the radio from Eggelton and directed the fire of the gunships that were on station. The cobras immediately fired into the wood line with their rockets and mini guns, suppressing the enemy fire, and forcing them to retreat. Jones carried Eggelton to the waiting chopper while Long, and Walden, provided covering fire into the wood line. Once Jones and Eggelton were safely on the chopper Long and Walden followed. The chopper lifted off without further incident. Division followed up with an infantry company who found twenty nine dead NVA soldiers on and around the trail. Long, Walden, and Jones were awarded the Silver Star for their action while Glaze received the Bronze Star. Sellens wounds were superficial but Eggelton and Rasen were seriously wounded. They spend months in the hospital undergoing physical therapy while recovering from their wounds. Fortunately both men would recover. Today, Rasen is a successful writer and Eggelton is an executive with Baush and Laum.

Radio relay was conducted using choppers, fixed wing, or anything else that would carry a LRRP and a radio to maintain communications with teams on the ground. Roy Barley had that duty on 17 February 1968. The morning had been a chore because the day before the fellow who was doing the radio relay for the first and last time, had really fouled things up, having teams plotted way out of position.

After checking the team's location and correctly plotting them on the map, they flew to assist Jones and Eggleton. Since the large LZ was real close to their location, Roy knew that he had to be real close on that. Jones came up on the radio and told Roy that they had "rough peanut butter" (meaning enemy activity) and that they should leave the area because they were spooking them. They flew a short distance away and continued to monitor the situation. Barley double checked the other teams to insure they were fine and then flew around the location for about 45 minutes in case of contact.

Barley was told by the pilot that they needed to return to Bearcat and refuel. Roy told him he was not happy to be returning to the landing strip while there was a team with bad guys around. He was told that if they did not refuel they would be on the ground with them. Roy advised the TOC and down they went.

The fix wing was in the middle of refueling when a jeep came roaring up and told them that they had to get back in the air ASAP. There was a team in heavy contact and Jones and Eggleton needed support right away. The Pilot had barely put in half of the needed fuel. Barley was in the back seat of the aircraft double checking the team's location. He noticed when they landed the pilot had taken the firing levers off the white phosphorus rockets. He had no time to mention to him that he forgot to re-arm the rockets. There were only four left as that morning they made a run on a bunker.

When they got back in the air, Barley called for artillery and advised that he would direct. The only guns that could reach the location were in Bearcat and that's where the gunships and pickup ships were coming from. Roy was advised that they could not fire over the choppers so he requested some fast movers but the ETA was considerably longer than the gunships. Talk about Frustration! He could see the fire team and slicks but could not make them move any faster.

Roy asked the pilot to fire some WP rockets and that is when he realized that the rockets were not armed. He directed the pilot to fly over the wood line where, based on the radio traffic, the bad guys were. When he did, Roy pulled the pins and threw out a couple frags. The aircraft took a couple of hits by small arms fire but nothing close to serious damage. The gunships hit station about then and really worked over the bad guys.

The rest of the day was uneventful and the other teams had no problems in the area. As soon as they touched down Roy wanted to find out if everyone was all right. That is when he learned Eggleton had been hit in both legs by an AK 47.

Enemy mortars and rockets struck Bearcat for the first time on February 27, 1968. Casualties and damage was extremely light as nine rockets and two mortars hit the base camp between 1:00 AM and 1:15 AM. Small arms contact was reported from one sector of the perimeter. The division's reaction was quick with light fire teams on station and 256 rounds of artillery fire returned.

All Cities were off limits, but if you stayed out of trouble, the military police would generally ignore you. One afternoon in May, Lieutenant Henry Hester, J.W. Boles, Hilan Jones, Herbert Vaughn, along with Kenneth Marze, drove to Mei Tho in the Lt's jeep. They were in one of the local bars when the local police made a raid. All except Vaughn were apprehended. The rest were taken to the local police station and told to wait in the courtyard for the MP's. Vaughn

Bonding of Warriors

had escaped but had the key to the padlock securing the chain locking the steering wheel on the jeep.

Not wanting to answer for a report from the MP's, Lt. Hester took out his pistol and shot the lock off the chain (it took three rounds). Everyone jumped in the jeep and headed out of town back to Dong Tam. Vaughn made it back to base camp on his own, long before the others. All is well that ends well and no reports were filled out that day.

When First Lieutenant Dale Dickey took command from Captain Clarence Matsuda the company was still designated 9th Division LRRPs. A few months after it was changed to Company E, 50th Infantry, Airborne/Ranger and stayed that way for just short of a year, when it was again re-designated. The company was now Company E 75th Rangers. Dale has the bragging rights of being the last LRRP commander, the only E 50th Infantry commander and the first E 75th Ranger Commander. The missions really started to change when General Ewell took command of the 9th Division. He believed in the unique capabilities of the Rangers and knew that they could be his eyes, ears, and yes muscle, when he needed it most. The G-2 Colonel Spiro was also a believer and supporter of the Rangers.

Dale's earliest memories of being the commander was that of being alone without Rick Stetson's calming effect and of not having Captain Matsuda's confidence, vast experience and leadership to fall back on in a tight spot. Here he was almost all alone in charge of guys like Jones, Frost, Dunlop, Nizialek, Walden, and the rest of the mob. One very peaceful morning sitting in his office thinking how great it was that all the teams were quiet, he was interrupted by First Sergeant Melvin Jones who announced that a very angry Major wanted to talk with him. As the Major entered the office he was yelling at the top of his lungs that he would have the entire company sent to jail and Dale relieved of his command if he did not discipline these two disrespectful NCO's.

From the brief description, he knew the Major was speaking of Frost and Jones. Thank God Dunlop was in the field. It appears they had been drinking and according to them it was just a little beer. They were on stand-down enjoying the amenities of the NCO Club and were walking back to the unit. They took a shortcut across the Major's yard, which had been recently seeded and was growing beautiful, lush grass, just like at home in Virginia. When he yelled at them to get off his grass, they responded with something like Yea! Yea! Yea! Not realizing or caring that he was a Major.

The Major went on to say that Jones became very disrespectful to him. By the time Jones and Frost were standing in front of their commander providing him with the facts as they knew them to be true. Their version in no way or manner matched with the Major's story and of course Jones denied being disrespectful. The Major stated that Jones threaten to "Smash him if he didn't get out of his face." Jones' version was that he stated, "If he didn't get out of his face, SIR" and Frost remembered the exact same thing, go figure.

The Major was in a t-shirt and Dale asked him how he was dressed when the confrontation happened. The Major when crazy at which time he was invited to leave the company area as it was really off limits to unauthorized personnel. He left and went to division to see Col. Ira A Hunt who told him to stay completely away from the Ranger compound and to remove his grass. Hunt told him that if dirt and mud were good enough for General Ewell it was good enough for the Major. Jones and Frost didn't get off completely but it set the picture for things to come for new inexperienced company commander. Dale commanded other units during his military career and no one threw anything at him that he hadn't seen as commander of the Rangers.

Specialist Four William Francis "Ski" Piaskowski was wounded on March 14, while on a routine patrol in Vinh Long Province with Sergeant Herbert Lee Vaughn, Staff Sergeant Hilan Jones, Staff Sergeant Herbert Cornelius Frost, and several others. The patrol was inserted from a Navy Patrol Boat (PBR) and was conducting a search for any signs of enemy activity. At mid-day they came upon a hooch that gave the appearance of being occupied. It was a normal abode for the area, complete with the hard packed floor and measured about twenty feet by thirty feet. Contained in the hooch were the normal Vietnamese furnishings. You could smell the incense and burnt charcoal, signs that the place was definitely occupied. Security was put in place and the hooch was searched for enemy weapons, equipment, and any other signs that would give an indication as to the status of the occupants.

A lone VC came down the trail, right into the Ranger position. He fired one round before running from the area. The Rangers returned fire immediately, but the VC was able to escape. That one round found its mark and hit "Ski" in the chest. Vaughn applied first aid to the chest wound and the team leader called for medical evacuation. Piaskowski was dusted off in short order and prognosis from the medical staff at the field hospital was good. We were all relieved to learn that "Ski" would make it. That evening word came from the hospital that he had died. Feelings of sorrow, anger, and frustration ran through the company area that night. The LRRP's had lost their fifth man after getting him home and thinking that he was going to be all right.

On 13 April, team leaders Specialist Four Robert J. Wallace, 19, from Saint Paul, Minnesota, and Sergeant Steven G. Averill, 21 from El Cajon, California were heading up a reconnaissance patrol in a suspected infiltration area near Bearcat. "We were just starting to set up about five yards off a trail when all of a sudden there they were, said Wallace. We were in heavy foliage when four VC came down the trail, from the west and four more from the east. When they spotted one of our men we opened up. We usually try to avoid that type of contact but when a VC is looking at you from fifteen meters away, you have to shoot," They had watched the trail for two days and nights, charting movement and numbers. On the third day they decided to grab one of the small groups which frequented the area. The four VC coming from the west looked perfect but then four others appeared from the east. They were the point element for about thirty more. "We killed five in the first burst and were pulling back toward the landing zone when the larger force hit, "continued Wallace.

Wallace said the VC fired small arms and automatic weapons at the team. Averill called in for gunship support. The gunships were on location within minutes and their fire was devastating. They were credited with killing ten VC. The LRRP's had been pinned down but the quick reaction and support of the choppers allowed them to break contact and escape to the LZ. The team was extracted without incident.

"1968"

Sometime during late March of 1968, Team 11 was called upon to go on a mission to observe a major north/south trail that crossed an east/west trace cut out by a jungle Destroyer. Word was that a major VC force was planning to attack a fire base on the south side of the trace.

Team 11 which consisted of team Leader Steve Cooper, Assistant Team Leader Danny Austin, point man Duane "Poncho" Alire, a new guy and Dan Bien, were inserted on the trace and moved off to the north side to pick up the trail.

On the way to the trail the going was slowed due to it being the dry season, and the team set up a night defense position before reaching the trail. The next day the team intersected the trail and followed it parallel off to one side for a while. Steve stopped the team and said, "With all the noise we were making we may as well get on the trail," which everyone knew was a major no-no. It did speed up progress somewhat, and about noon Bien got an uneasy feeling and told Austin they needed to stop. Cooper asked what was wrong and Bien told him things just didn't feel right. He got the map and said that the trail jogged to the right up ahead and that there was a stream a couple hundred meters ahead of them so they could fill their canteens. Again, Bien told him that he felt uneasy, so with it being so close to noon, they got off the east side of the trail about ten meters and started to get set up.

Just as soon as they got off the trail, Bien was down on one knee with his rucksack still on, facing east with the new guy seated facing north, Cooper was seated facing west, Austin was on his knee facing south and Poncho was on his knees facing north where he could look up the trail before it jogged, when the VC started coming down the trail toward them. They heard movement to the east of them parallel to the trail. They later figured that it must have been a flanking group. Poncho was looking at Cooper holding up his fingers to show how many. Cooper got on the radio to give a sit-rep to their tactical operations center. After forty or so walked by, they stopped. The team thought their goose was cooked as it got real quite. Then the VC started to eat lunch as it was about "pot time" (between noon and 2 p.m.). They threw their garbage toward them almost hitting some of them with their cans and wrappers.

About that time, the people back at the base alerted headquarters of the team's plight, and they requested one of the LRRPs sent to the Division Command Center to run the radio relay. They sent "Jonsey." They also sent a slick and two gunships, just in case.

The VC started moving and was heavily armed. They were obviously preparing to attack the fire support base, to the teams south. As the helicopters flew over the team's position to get a look, the VC would dive into the bush almost on top of the team. Cooper finally requested that the choppers back off so the VC could pass by. Two hours had passed before the end of the column passed the team. Everyone was cramped up from holding their position that they could hardly move. Poncho said that there was over a hundred VC in the column, not counting how many were in the flanking units.

Meanwhile, an S-2 (Intelligence) Major asked "Jonsey" what the team was up to, and "Jonsey" quipped, "I think they're going to fix bayonets and charge ...Sir." Cooper called in to let them know the count and kind of weapons that they were carrying and that that had finally passed the team. Artillery was directed from the choppers, but was limited, as there was a team on the south side and their radio was not working so the Forward Observer could not locate them. Finally, the team had a chance to eat lunch and relax somewhat. They stayed in their position not knowing in which direction the artillery had scattered the VC. The word was that they were seen crossing the trace, and that they were still on the team side of it. The team figured that the VC would cross at night and put the radio-less team in harm's way. They were wrong.

About 10:00 P.M, the VC started a sweep of the jungle knowing that someone had to be out there to call in their location for the artillery. They came back up the trail toward the team's position. Cooper called in another sit-rep with the team's location remaining in place. Soon they could hear the 1-0 five MM guns at the fire support base going off and illumination rounds lighting up the sky. Cooper called in a cease fire, again trying to let the VC pass them by. The VC completely infiltrated the teams position, walking right threw them, and continued north, possibly to a base camp of theirs.

The team was contacted very early the next morning to be at the trace at 8 A.M. for pick up. What had taken them better than a day and a half to come, took them thirty minutes, running as fast as they could through the jungle to get to the trace. With all the noise they made, they were happy that the VC had gone to their north.

The choppers came in as they popped a smoke grenade. It was such a relief to get out of that area and head back to base camp. Sometime later on another mission, they did locate their base camp, and another marathon run through the jungle to a landing zone ensued. But, on this morning, it was a great feeling to be alive.

Personnel had changed since they had gone to Nha Trang, and with Steve Copper ready to rotate back to the world, Team 11 would need a new leader. Sgt. Walden had thought enough of, and had enough confidence in "Poncho" that he made him 11's team leader, and Dan Bien was to tag along as his assistant. During this time there was apparently an "exchange program" with the "Aussies" as the team had two of them working with them.

Team 11's first mission was to go into an area where just the day before a team was compromised and upon extraction had dropped an M-79. They were to go in, complete the mission and try to recover the weapon. The team consisted of "Poncho," the two "Aussies," Astor Pagan, and Dan Bien. The area was just north of the perimeter wire surrounding Bearcat.

The team was inserted by chopper and was uneventful. They patrolled until "pot time" and stopped for lunch and a break. After eating his lunch Astor stretched on his side and crashed out for a little while. About that time the rest of the team was getting ready to "saddle up," one of the "Aussies" had noticed that a snake had slithered up along Astor's back and was laying parallel to him. It was a bamboo viper, the first they had seen in the bush. They "gently" woke Astor up, told him not to make any sudden moves until they told him. He wanted to know what was wrong. When they told him to roll to his front as fast as he could, one of the "Aussies" dispatched the snake with his knife.

That would have been enough excitement for one day if they hadn't been compromised by a couple of wood cutters about an hour later.

They were close to the location where the M-79 was lost. They tried to evade the wood cutters as best they could and set up their defensive night position.

It hadn't been dark an hour when they started getting mortared by the VC from the north and east of their position. To make matters worse, some arty battery at Bearcat, to their south, started in on H&I on top of their location. There were tree branches leaves and dirt clods flying all over the place. "Poncho" got on the horn to at least get our people to stop firing on their position. It seemed like an hour, but in reality only 10 or 15 minutes in duration the "BOOM-BOOM" finally stopped. A minute later, one of the "Aussies" shook off all the debris on top of him, looked over at "Poncho "and said "Thanks, Yank!" Needless to say, the team was extracted early the next morning. They never know if the M-79 was ever recovered, but all of them were just glad to be out of there!

On April 16, 1968, a mission was sent down for two teams to set an ambush in an area around the Binh Son Plantation, where in the preceding weeks there was sightings of heavy enemy activity. Team one was made up of "Top" Joseph Melvin Jones, SSGs Johnston Dunlop and Greg Nizialek, with Specialist Four Phil Katsis, Mattie Mathews and James Counts. Team two consisted of Specialists Four Wayne Fentress, Jack Delaney, Eugene Richardson, Richard "Little Jonesy" Jones, and George E. Kozach Jr. filling out the team. The teams hoped to ambush, and disrupt the movement of men and supplies in the area. Initial plans called for a 7:30 am insertion but unforeseen circumstances delayed them until almost 8:30 am. Behind schedule the teams were inserted and quickly moved to the selected position.

Team two was on the left flank of the ambush where Fentress and Richardson began putting the claymores in place as Delaney, "Little Jonesy," and Kozach provided flank and rear security. The claymores on the left portion of the kill zone were in place and armed. Simultaneously Katsis was placing the claymores on the right flank of the kill zone, while Dunlop was to insert the blasting caps and arm them. "Top" Jones, Counts and Nizialek were providing all around security on the right flank.

Before the ambush was completely set the VC came into view of the men on the right flank of the ambush. Normally the VC parade down the trails with an **"I own the jungle"** attitude, weapons slung over their shoulders, singing and talking loudly. "Charlie" was alert this day. They came quickly, weapons at the ready, and spotted the LRRPs before entering the kill zone. Automatic weapons fire from both sides broke the quiet of the morning that day and when the smoke cleared "Top" Jones was dead, SSG Dunlop was seriously wounded, and SP 4 Counts was shot in the forehead.

The initial volley of small arms fire hit Katsis's ruck sack and set off a yellow smoke grenade. The blast of the claymores knocked Delaney into a tree. He turned and began to fire into the smoke on the right flank of the ambush. A VC near "Top" was looking directly at him and Delaney saw him and fired. "Five tracers in a horse shoe shape came at me, 1 knew 1 was dead, all I heard was Pop, Pop, Pop, Pop! To my surprise, I was still standing" said Delaney. Loading his fourth magazine into his M-16 he continued to fire as the smoke was starting to clear. There were six to eight dead VC laying on the trail.

Delaney was checking the trail to make sure all the VC were dead as the rest of the team was moving Counts and Dunlop to the LZ. Fentress, Nizialek and Delaney them pulled "Top's body down into the riverbed. About that time all hell broke loose!! It sounded like 100 VC were on line shooting at them. Bullets were flying everywhere. Trees were cut down by the heavy volume of small arms fire, RPGs, and grenades!! The only thing between them and the VC was the riverbed. They dragged "Top's body down the riverbed, placed him under some overhanging brush, then camouflaged and booby trapped his body. They were unable to bring "top" out, but would return later to retrieve him. They low crawled for over 100 yards to the LZ!

At the LZ Fentress had them consolidate their magazines into a pile. Two were loading and shooting into the wood line. Delaney carried 31 HE rounds for his M-79 grenade launcher, using it as a mortar with the rounds hitting 50 to 100 yards into the wood line. Specialist Fentress applied a field dressing to Dunlap's wounds and administered morphine as they moved to the LZ for extraction. Delaney carried Dunlop to the chopper. Once aboard the chopper Dunlop succumbed to his wounds. A door gunner shot three VC that ran out onto the LZ. As the gunships rolled in, the team marked the enemy positions with tracer rounds. Rockets devastated the wood line and the pick-up chopper came in at tree top level, swooped down, and successfully extracted most of the patrol. Fentress and Mathews waited on the LZ for the second pick up chopper.

Unaware that there were two LRRPs left on the ground the VC emerged onto the LZ to scrounge any equipment or supplies that may have been left behind. Fentress and Mathews were able to direct the gunships and called in effective fire on the unsuspecting VC. Once back at Bearcat the choppers were refueled, while a reaction force made up from the Aero Rifle Platoon assembled on the helipad. They were guided back to the "combat zone" by Fentress. Two additional VC were killed while "Top's remains were recovered. Delaney was hit in the leg with shrapnel.

In early May of 1968 Roy Barley was notified of a mission to set up an ambush on one of the crossing canals on Thoi Son Island and then go to the eastern point of the island to check out another possible ambush site. The team infiltrated at high tide at night. This time a seven man team, with one new guy (Sgt Todd) and this was his first mission. It seemed that the team got in without alerting the locals. They stayed at the ambush site all night and had no activity at all on the water. Wrong canal for that night.

Morning came early, or as soon as the sun came up. The LRRPs moved out silently on their way to the site they were to check out. They had been trained to keep their eyes moving for targets while they moved at a slow pace as to make no noise. Silent and deadly. They came to a small hill on the island and headed down to the shore line to continue to the spot they were supposed to check out. Barley was the ATL on this mission and last in line. Roy caught some strange movement to the left and behind the hooch. The team member in front of him was seasoned veteran Sgt. Jim Glaze. Roy managed to get his attention and motioned that he had just seen a VC. He kept his weapon trained on the spot where the VC was, while Sgt Glaze moved off in a different direction to try to flank the VC. Gaze was successful on moving without the VC seeing him. Roy had seen the VC with a rifle before, but did not see one now. When he stood up and shouted to him to surrender (Choi Hoi) his eyes were as large as they could possibly be. His hands shot up and there was no doubt he was giving up. While Sgt Glaze searched him Roy radioed the team leader to advise him that they had taken a prisoner and was heading to his location. The PBR was called to shore to pick up the prisoner, and the team continued to the objective of the mission.

As Roy arrived at the PBR, a booby trap was pointed out to him and Sgt Glaze. A cluster of five grenades of the round baseball shape. They had just gotten this very new weapon and here was a cluster of five that the VC had gotten. How the hell where they able to obtain this new weapon? Jim and Roy had just passed them when they heard the distinctive buzz of a round passing across their faces and at the same time a couple of rounds kicked up dirt near them. They had just walked into an ambush. They reacted as they had been trained firing into the ambush. Roy knew that they were vulnerable on their flanks. He ran down the beach to a break wall on his left and popped up on the flank. He had noticed before they were ambushed that there was a beached boat that he thought would make good cover but was concerned that a VC might jump out and fire down the line. He had his M79 grenade launcher and sent a round into the boat and now the threat was gone. He turned his eyes to the ambush where the VC had run from the area. Having the grenade launcher allowed him to use it as a mortar tube and lobbed some high explosive in their direction. They went fourth as a team to check for any signs or whatever might be around. Blood trails…a couple of them. The team had inflected some damage, but so did they. Sgt Todd running his first mission, caught two rounds. One through his wrist and spleen and the other round went into his lower abdomen. He was bleeding big time and they called for a dust off and were told that it was on the way. They hurriedly took Sgt. Todd to the PBR and when the PBR was in the middle of the river a basket was lowered and Sgt. Todd was on his way the 3rd Surgical Hospital at Dong Tam and went straight into surgery.

On the island they were really pissed off. They looked for any telltale sign of where the VC might be. They came to a spot where there were bandages with fresh blood and obviously someone had been treated there. While there, something did not feel right and they fired off rounds where ever they thought the VC might hold out. The team leader had called for the Navy gunships (The Sea Wolfs) to work over the area and the team had to get to the boats and leave. The gunships worked over the area and watching the shredding of the trees, Roy knew that whoever was on the ground had no chance of survival.

Sitting on the boat watching the show was time to reflect on what had happened. Roy was almost out of ammunition and had only a couple of CS gas grenades left. He turned to look at their prisoner and saw that he was not in the best of shape. I guess a couple of guys had "fallen" off the motor cover into the well where the prisoner was held. His head was swollen to one side and looked strange. As they headed to Dong Tam the men were truly pissed off and wanted to go back to the island to search for those who had ambushed them. Already some line units were sweeping the area. They were thankful that they had called in and gave a good description and location of the booby trap.

When they reached the docks in the harbor and tied up, a rather pompous, new in country intelligence officer told us he was there to pick up the prisoner. When he saw the prisoner he wanted to know who had mistreated him. No one spoke up. He then asked who was in charge. Jim Glaze was the ranking member of the team, but not the team leader or assistant team leader, and he stepped forward saying the prisoner was his. We wore no rank so the Major had no idea as to who we were. He started to berate Jim and at that point I used my stupid mouth to tell the officer that it was obvious he did not want our prisoner and we were going to keep him. I heard a telltale metal sound of rounds being chambered by my teammates. This new in country intelligence officer had just learned to leave as alone.

Their ride back to their area had been waiting and he started up his engine. This officer had two MP's with only side arms with him and he seemed stunned and unable to decide what action to take. This was his introduction to the LRRPs of the 9th Infantry Division. They loaded the prisoner and headed to their area where he was interrogated by their interpreter. The Navy SEALs wanted a shot at the prisoner too. They radioed them to meet them at the docks to hand over the prisoner. The LRRPs liked to work with the Navy more than the Army. As they were standing at the dock talking to the Navy guys, some people were eyeing them with strange looks. They realized they had not gotten cleaned up yet and were a nasty site with dried blood, muddy and torn clothing and the remains of camouflage. There was a mass shower that they headed to and went in and took showers fully clothed. The mud and crap came off and they did feel better. They went to their company area to peel off the clothing and send them to the laundry. As they sat around discussing the mission word came back from the SEALs that the prisoner had confessed to being part of the ambush and he was to be the bottom of the L shaped ambush. Turns out that Roy had no reason to be concerned about their right flank. If the prisoner had not been captured he would have been able to fire down the line and almost surely they would have suffered some serious damage.

That evening they heard that Todd was out of surgery and doing well. They headed over to the 3rd Surgical Hospital and managed to find him sitting up in bed and eating ice cream. Damn, I had no idea that ice cream was available. Sgt. Todd called his nurse and asked if his teammates who saved his life could also get some ice cream. Todd told them he was going home and would be medically retired. He had received the million dollar wound and thanked them for saving his life. Their ice cream showed up and guys started joking around. Things were getting serious and they did not need that. Roy asked whose turn was it to get wounded next. If they worked it right they could have ice cream after every mission. No one volunteered. Just plain dumb luck.

Sargent Sal Di Sciascio recalls a close call from friendly fire while on this "routine mission:" I had taken my team on what was a routine hide and observe mission. I had 4 Americans and one Vietnamese PRU.

The chopper had dropped us off without incident after a series of "swoop and squat" false landings and we had set up in a small tree line. The area was very open with clumps of small trees around the perimeter. Shortly after we settled in I noticed a LOH cruising overhead. He was dropping to get a better look at the area. Since my team did not look like conventional soldiers, I ordered them to hunker down because I knew that LOH's rarely flew alone. I got on the radio and asked Higher what the hell they were doing in my AO and to please un-ass the area.

Then, from a clump of tall grass about 50 meters away, a young VC jumps up and fires a burst with his AK at the LOH, to no effect, I might add. I thought to myself, "Oh Shit... Here it comes!!!" Just then a Cobra came out of the Sun and opened up on the VC with his mini gun. The seemingly solid stream of red tracers masked the 4 ball rounds. The VC disintegrated in a cloud of red mist that was his blood, meat and bone. I watched as he blew away like a dandelion flower in a wind. I knew what was next. I ordered the team to lay head to toe in a parallel to the edge of our cover. The cobra raked the area near where the VC had been then slowly wheeled and peppered the perimeter of the clearing with red hell. We watched as the ground churned up about 5 meters from us...then it was quit as the two choppers casually left the area. I can confirm that whoever he was, he'd seen his last Tet. We did patrol the area later but I shied away from that particular place. If there were any more enemy in the area, I'm thinking that they are probably still running north.

Souvenirs were a big thing. Everyone wanted to recover a weapon or some other war trophy to take home. Marze recalls the mission on 25 May, 1968. He, Vaughn, Ralph Harter and three others were tagged for a patrol on Thoi Son Island, just a thousand meters or so from Dong Tam in the middle of the Mekong River. Vaughn briefed the patrol emphasizing that there would be a lot of tin VC flags nailed to the trees throughout the area and to leave them along. They would be booby-trapped. Charlie knew that the GI was curious and sometimes careless.

That afternoon the navy crew picked the patrol up and would insert them just before dark. Just after dark the team off loaded from the PBR onto Thoi Son Island and moved quickly and quietly across a rice paddy for about 600 meters. The patrol moved into a tree line, set their security, and continued to monitor the area. The following morning the patrol moved out through some thick Nipa palm and came upon a well-used trail. They spotted several tin VC flags nailed to the trees. Marze was about15 meters behind Vaughn who ignored his own advice, taking one of the flags and pulling it from the tree. It was booby trapped. The explosion caught Vaughn in the chest. He was killed instantly (he only had 40 days before going home) the loss of Vaughn still haunts Marze today, some 35 years later.

After a couple of months with the SEALs, Marze returned to the LRRPs who, in between missions, were in the middle of constructing their living area at Dong Tam. Having left a super living area at Bearcat: hooch's had tin roofs, wooden sides about four feet off the ground, wire mesh the remaining couple of feet to the roof and were set on concrete slaps. They were in the process of building even a better one. The LRRPs were a creative bunch and sometimes acquired building material outside of the normal requisition process. The limber used to build the small club in the company area was gotten by of "midnight requisition." Marze, (and a few others) acquired some particle board and Masonite that was intended for constructing the base chapel. The Chaplain caught them in the act and required them to attend services or he would report them. They attended the required amount of services, returned the acquired lumber and nothing more was said. Sometime during this construction, Marze used the phrase, "you lantern head-son-of-a -bitch," He was immediately tagged with the nickname "Lantern head," by which he still answers today.

On May 14, 1968, Patrol Leader Staff Sergeant James Glaze, Australian Special Air Service (SAS) trooper by the name of Duffy, Specialist Four Larry J Styer and Charles Knight, along with two or three others (one was a new guy), were on a mission in the Dinh Tuong Province. They were working with an Infantry Brigade which was being hit by sniper fire as they transported supplies along a highway in the "Pink Palace" area. The mission of the LRRP team was to search for and take out the snipers. Late in the afternoon the LRRP's met up with a line platoon that would be providing support.

Immediately after linking up with the support element, they saw approximately 10 VC moving across an open area in the rice paddy to the front. The team left the line platoon to intercept and block the route the VC was taking. The team moved through a line of woods and along a dike covered in heavy vegetation in their attempt to cut off the VC. As they started to cross the canal, they began receiving small arms fire from across the canal to their right front.

The Australian had gotten across prior to the team receiving fire and was called back across the canal to join the rest of the patrol. As he crossed back to the friendly side, fire was received from the front, the left, and the right of their position. Judging from the volume of fire, there had to be more than the 10 VC originally spotted. The LRRP team returned fire and Glaze called for the line platoon to move up to their position as he simultaneously called in artillery. The line unit was not able to move forward.

The new guy's weapon jammed and Glaze moved over to assist him. Trading weapons, Glaze was able to clear the jam and continued to call in artillery. Shortly after the enemy fire ceased, the line platoon joined up. The area was searched and blood trails were found as well as other signs that the VC had entered the canal before disappearing. The men searched for a tunnel opening in the bank of the dike but could not find anything. The team was extracted without further incident.

It happened on 1 June, 1968 in a flat open see-for-miles rice paddy in the Plain of Reeds. Kenneth McConkey witnessed a young buck sergeant by the name of J.W. Boles back down a Bird Colonel who was abusing the use of the LRRPs that day. The Colonel's idea was to send seven LRRPs out a mile to a mile and a half ahead of the rifle company they were attached to for the purpose of drawing enemy fire. They were then to keep the fight going until he foot-slogged with the company across this distance of open rice paddy country to make a full engagement.

J.W. spoke quietly and diplomatically, but the message was clear that he considered it a categorically stupid idea and it wasn't going to happen with his team. Boles starting out with "Sir, I don't know if you've ever worked with the Long Range Patrol before, but…." This went on for maybe five minutes with Boles talking sense and the Colonel getting more and more insistent. He realized that Boles wasn't going to budge and he finally just stood and glared. You could just see the dreaded words dangling on the tip of the Colonel's tongue.....but he didn't say it because he knew Boles was not about to be intimidated.

No telling what Boles was ready to say to the Colonel while they were having their stare-down, but by the way the conversation had escalated, one could guess that instead of the firm but respectful tone he had maintained it was probably going to be along the lines of "Sir, that's dumb and we're just not going to do it,....and if you don't like it, call the General and see what he thinks of your idea." They stood eyeball to eyeball for about a half a minute and then the Colonel backed up and walked away mumbling something about "Well, if you're not going to do your job…" A few minutes later he came back and split the team up and distributed them among the platoons as an insult for him to save a little face out of the deal, but at least the LRRPs didn't provide Charlie with a casual afternoon of target practice like the Colonel wanted.

A few minutes later the word came down that "Somebody spotted a few gooks in some woods and were going to flush them out and shoot them like pheasants.: They put the company in choppers and flew into the Plain of Reeds. McConkey hit the ground in the middle of what appeared to be a battalion-sized firefight on three sides of him. That "Leader of men" got a lot of brave soldiers killed for no good reason that afternoon. McConkey personally heard the Colonel give the Company Commander orders to assault. He kept hollering "You've got to assault those positions."

The company was pinned down and losing more guys by the minute while he was high and dry up 3000 feet in his helicopter right above us. Another of his companies was trapped inside the NVA base camp getting the shit shot out of them. He just kept screaming that they had to move forward. There was no cover and little concealment against well-fortified positions and they were chopping the company up at will with .51 caliber machineguns.

Without using the word he was calling the guys under Lt O'Reilly's command cowards and they knew they weren't. What he was telling them to do was simply a military impossibility. At one point McConkey looked up at the chopper thinking, "You ignorant son of a bitch if you really think this can be done why don't you come on down here and grab a rifle there's plenty of them laying around." The next morning there were 39 bodies loaded on the choppers.

McConkey has the bullet with his name on it as a reminder of his action. Working along the battle line hoping to link up with some of the rest of his team, (Boles had already gone back to be dusted off after getting hit in the leg) he came upon the scene previously described, with the C.O., a platoon leader and about a platoon's worth of guys all bunched up pinned down getting the shit shot out of them. No LRRPs in sight, so he was first going to pass on through and keep looking for Smitty, MacCallum, Marz or Taitano.

Then on the opposite side of the group he spotted a kid named Johnny Carpenter that they had met the night before when Boles team bed down next to his squad. McConkey had confidence in him, and figured that if he couldn't find any LRRPs, at least he could hook up with him and maybe Mike Chubbuck. The platoon was so bunched up that he didn't want to crawl right thru them drawing attention to the movement and get somebody else shot. That was happening regularly enough as it was.

He detoured around the front.... crawling and sliding sideways to keep the narrowest profile towards the front and not expose any more target profile than necessary. He would move a couple feet whenever the .51's stopped to catch their breath a bit, (the AK fire remained steady) so it was pretty slow going. As luck would have it, just when he got to the middle of the front, the intensity picked up and he was stuck there for a quite a while trying to be small....you all know what trying to be small means.

While lying there listening to LT. O'Reilly trying to talk this Colonel out of making another futile, suicidal charge, it dawned on him that the top of his head was by default the furthest point of advancement. He had categorically the front row seat, though that had not been his original intent. He was just trying to go around the group. This was not a movie, not a dream, not a drill, it was actually happening. It sounds silly. But it's God's honest truth... the corny poetic words came into his mind "At any second a bullet could come crashing into my brain." Yes, "crashing"...he didn't know what it was all about, just that it happened.

Nobody was moving or firing back at them for 15-20 minutes. A few small movements as a new angle of fire came through...trying to get a little better concealment, but basically they were just lying there getting shot, while O'Reilly tried to talk sense to that S.O.B. Colonel up in the air. There was so much lead coming through that if you hadn't gotten hit where you were you didn't really want to roll the dice by moving to a new spot.

So the only thing he could think of after the brain crashing vision was to get his head lower. Scooping about a half a basketball's worth of the ground he made a mini foxhole for his head. It started to ooze water into the bottom of the hole, (this soft mushy ground is what undoubtedly saved his life when he had fallen out of the chopper a couple hours earlier), so he took off his beret and lined the hole with it, keeping his right eye just above ground level to be able to see forward.

No more than a minute later it felt like someone had given his small pack (they weren't carrying rucks) a hell of a kick and it kind of raised him up out of the hole a bit. Knight's platoon leader, Lt. Jones, had been lying with his hand on his thigh with his head behind the pack. He could feel him moving occasionally to peek around during short lulls in the firing. Jones said "My God, I just got hit in the head with a bullet and I'm still alive!"

McConkey replied, "Ya, that must be the one that just went through my pack." It had hit the buckle on the top of his pack, gone through, come out the bottom mostly spent and went "klink: on the forehead of the platoon Leaders helmet and fell straight down and stuck to the back of his hand, burning him. He shook it off onto the ground and then picked it up. He said "I've got it right here in my hand, it's still hot!" Without taking his head out of the hole he reached back with his left hand and hit him on the shoulder, holding out his hand like a bellboy for a tip. He put it in his hand and it wasn't hot anymore, but still had warmth. McConkey placed it in his shirt pocket.

Many further events unfolded and the next day when they were flown out of there to a camp with buildings and stuff, Jones was coming into the toilet/washroom just as McConkey was leaving. He said, "Say, you still have that bullet? That's my bullet, you know." McConkey replied, "Your bullet, Sir?" "Yeah, that hit me right in the head, you know." He told him "Well, sir, I look at it this way, if it hadn't hit the buckle on the top of my pack and lost its punch,...I wouldn't know it, .. and you wouldn't care. And since I did get my head out of the way, if it hadn't hit the buckle on the top of my pack and lost its punch,... you'd have the bullet, you wouldn't know it, and I wouldn't care. As it is, we both know how it all came down, I got the bullet and I'm keepin' it... OK, sir?: He opened his mouth and raised his finger like he was going to make some point of logic, but then just shook his head and walked away.

McConkey wasn't really trying to f... with the guy because he truly respected him. He just wanted to keep the bullet. They had been on the scene together 3 or 4 times on June 1, and he really was a good and brave officer. The next day when O'Reilly got killed he took over the company. O'Reilly was a real pro, too. McConkey went to their area a couple weeks later to visit with Knight and Chubbuck to express his remorse for getting their buddy Carpenter killed. That's when he learned from Knight that Chubbuck had gotten killed the same day as O'Reilly...more of that fucking Colonel's doing. McConkey has the last picture taken of Michael Chubbuck. Bumping into LT. Jones, they talked a minute. Jones said that he had been walking right besides O'Reilly as he got stitched across the chest. He looked at Jones, and as he was falling said. "Well, you got it, Lieutenant." The guy held a change of Command ceremony on the way down to the ground...now there was a soldier. MacCallum remembers him, too. We'd have been proud to have either of them in the LRRPs.

Gary Beckham remembers that day as it forever burned deep into his head. Intelligence had picked up info than an NVA regiment had moved into the Plain of Reeds and they wanted to find them. They put together a plan involving several companies and mobile artillery that could be chopper'd into an area to provide devastating fire, but the artillery never showed up. The LRRPs went in as point for a couple of $2^{nd}/39^{th}$ companies, but soon got pulled out after no contact was made. The companies continued towards a tree covered rise; one company coming from one direction and another from another direction.

Beckham recalls that the team hung around the main gathering area and heard that one of the companies had run into the NVA encampment and has hit terribly hard. The CO was shot several times (but he lived). The company was surrounded and was being decimated. With that, everyone (LRRPs too) went to the battle. Our team went with a few line troops in a Huey; just before we set down the pilot said he was receiving fire, the LZ was hot and just below us a large explosion occurred in the bushes, raising a large cloud of brown silty dust. He remembers watching the face of a black private who was in the same chopper, and the look of his pale skin, almost white, told all that soon he was going to die.

The company we went with was pinned down. After laying on our bellies listening and watching blue tracers coming at us, we figured this was going to be a tough day. Our team jumped up and ran to a bush line for cover. I remember joking with the team and a couple of us rose up, just enough with our knees bent to see, but we didn't see anything but bushes and trees. Then almost immediately we heard snapping of the bushes we were hiding behind followed by blue tracers and the delayed report of the AK-47 aimed at us. I remember looking at the bush, seeing clearly where the bullets had ripped through the branches where we had just been standing.

We heard the company that first made contact, was somewhere between us and the NVA line, so we were instructed not to fire towards the pinned down company, so what were we there for? Could not fire at anyone!! We stayed put and I remember the company we were with sending a squad out to locate a trail. I noticed, as did just about everyone else, that the trees had a strange fruit hanging from them….. grenades everywhere…each one a booby trap with a tripwire. Pretty soon we heard limited firing……and troopers started dragging wounded comrades towards us. I and some other team members helped administer medical help to the wounded but it was pretty useless; each one (except for one lucky fellow with an upper wound) was shot point blank in the head….obviously from a sniper in a damn spider hole. I dragged one of the wounded to a wounded collection area, where bodies were lined up in a long, grotesque row. It was the black fellow from the chopper that had been shot through the temples….bullet went in one temple and exit was through the other…clean wound, no blood. But he was blind and in terrible pain. I held him in my arms for a while, for there was absolutely nothing that a medic or I could do. He kept saying, and I'll never forget this… "God, help me, I can't see, God help me!" Well God did relieve his pain for he died in my arms blind to the world forever.

At that point, I was no longer a boy or young man; in an instant, at the cost of the life of another, I matured into a man of intense caring for others and a stronger appreciation of all that lives…of everything I see. I could go on for hours remembering this action…..I remember being the only one to stand up at night with my strobe to direct the choppers in to pick up the dead and dying; I remember ducking blue tracers aimed directly at me for I must have looked like a lighthouse, a beacon for the NVA fire. I remember Lt Hester going to the hospital during the battle and walking the long line of the dead, dying and wounded, searching desperately for any LRRPs….fortunately, none of us was hit.

"RAIDERS FROM THE SKY"

BY

PESCOTT "PUCK" SMITH

In June, 1968, a special mission came down from Col Spirito at Division Headquarters. Lt. Prescott "Puck" Smith was chosen to lead the mission. The 9th Division communication network had been picking up suspected VC radio transmissions for a couple of weeks. Because the 9th Infantry had been able to pinpoint the messages with pretty much certainty and were convinced that the VC command network in the northeastern sector of IV Corps was controlled by this command structure, it was imperative that these radio messages be eliminated. Even though headquarters was able to monitor these transmissions and had the capability to locate where the messages were coming from sampans in the middle of various rivers in the Delta, any approaching vessel could be detected easily. By the time they might be boarded, the enemy would have time to get rid of the radio equipment before the friendlies could capture them. Col. Spirito came up with the idea of trying to intercept these sampans through the air instead of by boat. He felt that a LRRP team could somehow be inserted by helicopter.

Lt. Smith organized a team consisting of Sgt. Willie Boone, Kenneth Marze, Sgt. Hicks and Spec. Four Rodgers. This type of insertion had never been tried before so the team practiced by jumping from a helicopter to a moving two and a half ton truck. Lt. Smith requested that Capt. Bill McCreary be the helicopter pilot for this special mission, as he knew him to be an excellent pilot, and would operate well under the pressure of the mission.

The potential success of this operation was going to center around proper identification of the sampan that was transmitting the radio message; the ability of the pilot to fly the team to the sampan without being prematurely detected and the successful insertion of the LRRP team on the sampan.

As far as the insertion was concerned, this would be by far the most difficult LRRP insertion ever attempted. The pilot's skill as an aviator would really be tested, as he approached the sampan, flared the helicopter and brought it to a hover above the boat. Because the sampan would be moving, the closer the helicopter was to the boat was critical to the LRRPs being able to land successfully on the sampan deck. It was impossible to say with any certainly how far they would need to jump. Capt. McCreary told the team that if he could get them closer than ten feet, he would be doing well.

It would be five days before another VC transmission was confirmed and the LRRPs loaded a helicopter and headed for the sampan. Flying at tree top level, the chopper swooped in over the sampan as Cpt. McCreary pulled back on the controls of the chopper, the tail started to dip, the front of the chopper flared upward and the airspeed began to dramatically decrease. The next few seconds seemed to go in slow motion as the team jumped out of the chopper; they felt as if they were jumping into a wind tunnel. The drop was about eight to ten feet before they hit the deck of the sampan. As Lt Smith hit the deck he landed on his right side. He quickly recovered and saw a young Vietnamese man running toward the cabin which was located in the center of the boat. Before he could turn and look in the other direction toward the stern of the boat, he heard a burst of M-16 fire and turned as another Vietnamese man who was holding an AK-47 fell about five feet in front of him.

Sgt. Willie Boone yelled "I got the Fucker." As he swung around and looked at the other side of the boat, one of the other team members yelled, "Marze is in the water!!" Smith looked past the stern and in the wake of the sampan he could see Kenneth Marze in the water.

Luckily, one of the door gunners had seen him fall into the river and had communicated that to the pilot, so the helicopter was circling back around to pick him up.

Sergeant Hicks and Specialist Four Rodgers had already entered the sampan cabin and captured three enemy suspects and another guy appeared at the bow and walked toward them with his hands in the air. All of this activity transpired in just a few seconds and the boat was secured.

Even though they had one guy in the water it seemed like the insertion had gone very well. Hicks and Rodgers moved the three VC out onto the main deck and had forced them to lay face down with their arms stretched out in front of them. Sergeant Boone had secured the AK-47 of the VC that he had shot, and confirmed that he was dead. The other VC who had walked toward the main cabin from the bow stood frozen with his hands above his head and they could see the fear in his eyes.

"The radio is in the cabin," Sergeant Hicks yelled to Lt. Smith. Lt Smith entered the cabin and found a small table in the middle of the room with a radio transmitter on top of it. A cord running from the radio to the ceiling provided the antenna. A thorough search of the cabin produced another AK-47, two 45-caliber hand-guns, a small barrel of rice and a jug of water.

Within minutes, two PBRs came speeding in to tow the sampan to shore and pick up Marze who was waiting on the bank of the river. Hicks and Rodgers accompanied the prisoners back to Dong Tam on the chopper for interrogation while the rest of the team stayed aboard the sampan that was being towed to Nha Be. The team would later learn from the 9th Division G-2 interrogation team that, that the VC had been totally shocked by the insertion as they referred to the team as "the raiders from the sky."

Stand downs (the time between missions) and promotions were excuses to throw a party. "Lantern head" was promoted to SP4 in early July and to celebrate his promotion there was the usual "wash tub" fill of punch which consisted of a couple quarts of vodka mixed with grape fruit juice, fruit cocktail, and plenty of ice. This concoction was prepared by LT Hester in recognition of the promotion "Lantern head" would receive the following day. Everyone had over indulged and was not in the best of shape at the formation the next morning. Lt Hester called "Lantern head" to the front and told him to hit the ground and start pushing it up. He said it was for swearing at him the night before. "Lantern head" had done one push up when Lt Hester dropped the SP4 patch on his back and told him to get back in formation. Marze was now a proud SP4.

Lt. Henry R. Hester was a fine officer who cared deeply for his men. A lot of effort was made these past few years to locate him. The brotherhood of the LRRP/Rangers has lasted all these years. Several reunions have come and gone. More men have been located and communication has continued among those that have been located. It was sad to learn Henry passed away the 15th of September 1997, before he could be located. He will be remembered by all those that knew him.

In early July 1968, Roy Barley found himself on another mission in the Mekong Delta. He saw Frosty heading towards him like he had a purpose and not just to bullshit. His famous, (at least to him) handle bar mustache had no smile beneath it and he looked serious. Frosty sat down next to him and Roy just knew something was up and Frosty was not happy. Frosty was Herb Frost, one of the most colorful members of our unit and one excellent soldier and leader. In the field he was confident and had an attitude that no matter what came his way he could handle it. He hardly ever ran a mission with Frosty, but the few he had he really liked his actions in the field. Frosty told him that they were going to run a mission that the Division had requested. This was a fairly new area and there was almost no information on what the enemy strength, units, or weapons were. They decide that they could just walk out there and get them a prisoner.

We were going to go in heavy. Fred Wheeler and his PRU' with Jim Glaze as ATL. Frosty was the overall team leader and Roy had been assigned as a team leader with a team made mostly of new people. For a couple of them it was their first mission.

Frosty was going to do the over flight and handed him a map with their Area of Operations marked on the plastic that covered it. He gathered the men assigned and went over what they were going to do and then hooked up with Wheeler. Nothing special about this mission except for the fact that it would require three helicopters and that the insertion would draw attention. They all agreed that it could go bad very quickly and they would have to be on their toes. They were going to be inserted the next morning and all the men involved were going over weapons and equipment, getting a good meal, (hard to do with Army food) and a good nights' sleep (if at all possible).

Frosty returned from his over flight and he went over what he knew about the area from the air. They had adequate LZ's that they could be inserted into and extracted from and there was a new fire support base not a long ways away so they had artillery not far off. It looked about as good as it could be considering the mission.

First light saw them putting on camouflage, getting dressed in their tigers and generally insuring that they were ready. They always inserted at last light but this time it was different. Around 8 AM or so they headed to the flight line to board the birds that would take them to the LZ Frosty had picked out. Since they had moved to the Delta they no longer had the pilots of Delta troop 3/5th Cav and now just had only any pilot of the 9th Aviation. The 3/5th pilots were excellent and knew them and their missions. They went out of their way to insure that they got out of trouble when they stepped in it.

The air was relatively cool as high up as they were. By cool it had to have been around 80 degrees as opposed to the normal temperatures of 95 to 100 with high humidity. As Roy looked around he had a funny feeling that they were not going to insert where they were supposed to. The direction they were headed to now at tree top level did not look like the map. He radioed Frosty but as he did the bird flared and they were on their way out the door. The birds did not sit down at all and were gone in a flash. They checked to insure all men were there and in good shape. No warning shots and apparently they got in without drawing much attention.

Roy quickly moved his team to Frosty's location and Wheeler was there also. They had been dropped in the wrong area. They radioed the fire support base and asked for a marking round at where they were supposed to have landed. From where the air burst occurred he could tell they were a good four klicks away. They were not even in their AO. He called for another marking round at another location and from where it went off he had a pretty good idea as to where they were. They had to alert all friendly forces where they were so they would not light them up. They did that through the fire support base. And then informing the men on the mission one or two at a time. Gathering a group is not healthy in the field. They had a canal close so a decision was reached to follow that down to a small village.

They moved quickly and quietly into the village, and when the villagers came out of their hooch's they were shocked to see them. Roy had found a foot bridge (really a log) into the village that was situated in a bend of the trail. If anyone approached the log they would be in the center of the log before they could see into the village. A perfect spot to grab a prisoner.

He set up with men flanking each side of the log. About that time he caught movement up the canal and headed in that direction. An old man in a dugout was coming down the canal. He had him tie his dugout up and walked him over to where Wheeler and his PRUs were and asked them to treat him gently. The old man was given some American cigarettes, good food and sweets and that made his day. They could not just let him go after he saw them. He headed back to the team set up and as soon as he got there he could hear movement on the other side of the log. He watched as the young man who was military age hit the middle the log. His eyes opened as wide as his face. If he moved one way or another he was dead. The team had been told that if he opened up they were to open up too. His hands shot up into the air and he followed their directions. Roy ran him over to the PRU team for interrogation. Old Papason, enjoying good American cigarettes and sweets, started jabbering away. He headed back to the team. Larry Styer, who was the company clerk and wanted to go to the field, proved to make one excellent LRRP. He was fantastic in stepping out right beside him every time. Roy watched his eyes and Styer watched everything else. He made the job easy.

When he got back to the team he knelt down and kept his eyes and ears open for movement. The men covering the bridge were keeping their eyes and ears open and were ready for action, if needed. Their role in this operation was extremely important and they really were doing a great job. The knowledge of having this amount of fire power aimed at the log made his job easier. After about 5 minutes they had another military age man get to the mid-point of the log and Barley along with Styer stepped out. Again the total look of surprise, he had a small packet in his hand and dropped it into the water. He followed their instructions and was taken prisoner. Barley recalls the water as being more like a deep open sewer line. It stunk to high heaven and had a very nasty look about it. Styer said he was going in after the packet. The water and mud came to about his waist and the longer he stayed in there the higher it got as he sank in the mud. He got the packet on the second try. The packet was about 8 inches long and about 5 inches wide. It was wrapped in oil skin so it made the trip back with the prisoner to the PRUs and Wheeler for interrogation.

Returning to their positions at the log Barley and Styer waited for their next victim. They waited for about 15 minutes and suddenly had movement and noise from the other side of the log. It seemed like it happen in a flash. Suddenly there was another military aged young man in the middle of the log. Moving quickly they drew down on him. Barley stepped into the clearing and told him (in Vietnamese) to come here quickly. He looked like he may run, but that would have been fool hardy. His eyes kept darting around as if he was looking for a hole to dive into. When he saw that they were determined to capture him, he was not going anywhere. Barley reached out and pulled him across the log by his hair. He started to yell and Barley's hand went across his mouth and stifled any sound the prisoner meant to give. He just pissed Barley off. They made sure the team was on full alert because they though he may have been trying to warn someone who might be on the other side of the log. They were quite sure that there was someone there but did not want to blow their productive snatch site. They took his ass back to the PRUs and Wheeler.

Barley discussed the situation with Frosty and Wheeler and told them that he thought that they had worn out their welcome and needed to get out of there. Wheeler told him that the prisoner that they captured with the oil skinned packet was a North Vietnamese Lt and his shoulder boards and ID had been in the packet. They contacted the Fire support base and requested extraction from the area. No helicopters were available to extract them and they would get back to them, saying that they may have to stay the night where they were. They told them who they had captured and that staying out there was out of the question.

An armored column from another fire support base that was operating in the area was ordered to head their way. They would meet them out at the road about a klick and a half away. The team's only way out of the area was across the log where they had captured their prisoners and Roy let Frosty and Wheeler know that he thought that there might be bad guys on the other side of the log. Larry Styer decided to go across and check things out. As much as he did not want to go Roy could not let Styer go alone. They moved across the log quickly and carefully moved and checked out the area. It looked like some people had been there and now were nowhere in sight. They also checked for booby traps and it was clear so they motioned for the rest of the guys to come through.

Since the road was right in front of them, some distance away, they decided the best thing to do was to stay off the dikes and keep low. They moved right along until they got into the center of the field and then they heard the sound of rounds passing above them with an occasional green tracer mixed in. The shots were high so they got down. They continued to move but switched to the other side of the dike as it offered a bit more cover. When they did this they were greeted with rounds from the wood line on that side and these were a bit more accurate so back over the dike they went. Every other man was firing to one side or the other. They could see the muzzle flashes from each side and were putting accurate fire in those areas. About that time the armored column showed up and came up on our push asking if they wanted them to fire some rounds down range and into the enemy positions. Roy thought what a great idea and it would be fun to see what a tank could do. When Frosty told the tanks that their help was not needed as they would get themselves out by fire and movement. Roy got really pissed off. He came up on the radio and told Frosty in no uncertain terms that if they wanted to blow the shit out of the VC then they should be allowed to do so. There were some curse words involved but to no avail. Frosty told him to get the hell off the net and shut up. When Frosty was pissed it was best to just let it go and steer a wide berth. They did the fire and movement thing and at one point Roy stood up to get a better shot and accurately put fire into the muzzle flash. That stopped the shooting from one side, and they could move quickly to the road.

Roy had never ridden on an APC (armored personnel carrier) and had no idea as to what he was in for. They split the prisoners up and put one on each of the APCs. He climbed up on that infernal machine and off they went to the Fire Support Base. The ride was one that he will never wanted to do again. Damn machines were loud and it felt like it had a large bull's eye on the side of it. No place to hold on to and just had to hang on as it bumped and shook and rattled its way down the road. He could just see the letter to his parents now. "The Army regrets to inform you that your son was run over by an APC 'cause he could not hold on." At one point he looked over to the prisoner and was astonished to see him in his squatted position, with his hands tied behind him and blindfolded and just taking every jolt with his legs. Incredible.

They finally pulled up to the entrance of the fire support base. They had no idea as to what the name of it was but it was built into a cemetery. This was very strange, almost surreal. They dismounted those infernal machines and headed into the operations center for the brigade. There was quite a crowd gathered as the word got out about the capture of a North Vietnamese officer. On oddity that far south in the Delta. We heard the distinct sound of a helicopter coming in. They first thought that it was coming to pick them up so they could get back to their base camp. That thought was extinguished quickly as two cobra gunships and a single Huey came into view and landed. Out stepped a one star general and a photographer and a major from intelligence. The photographer asked who captured the prisoners, and the team pointed to Roy. He told the photographer that it was a team effort and without the other guys it wasn't possible. The photographer took his photo as he was talking with him and another team member took his picture at the same time from a different angle. The one star walked up and Roy motioned for Frosty and Wheeler to come over with Styer. Being in the field a salute was not required and if had been they wouldn't have given one any way. He could have brought enough helicopters to take us all back to the Division base camp. He, the major and his aides took all three prisoners back to the Division Base camp and they were stuck at this base camp for the night.

Fred Wheeler was smiling and Roy just had to ask why. It seems that his PRU's had gotten a ton of information from the prisoners. The officer they knew about and the other two prisoners were VC but what they did not know was they were both high ranking cadre who were involved in recruiting men to join their cause. Fred had radioed this to our CO who was going to bring it to the attention of the commanding general of the Division that evening. The one star did not even talk with Fred or his PRU's.

They settled in for the night at the fire support base. They had a bunker to rack out in, no beds no cots or anything like that, just the ground on top of graves. This was nuts! The mosquitoes got to them early so Roy climbed on top of the bunker for a good sleep. He went to sleep quickly and later found the entire team on the bunker asleep. In the early morning hours they heard an explosion near them and Roy saw sparks coming from the sound. He heard someone yell incoming and they all dove off the bunker and went back inside. Someone, laughing their ass off looked in on them and told them that it was the mortar section shooting and all the sparks were coming from the tubes being really worn. They were in no mood to laugh as all they wanted was some sleep.

In the morning the unit at this base had hot chow on and they went over to see if they could beg some. They had never seen green eggs before and decided that they would stick with the LRRP Rations that they had brought with them. A little C-4 to heat water, pour it in the pouch and let it sit for about 15 minutes and then throw on some Tabasco sauce and it made an edible meal. At least it wasn't green. About that time the team was informed that three birds were on their way to pick them up. A few minutes later they were on their way back to their base camp and a hot shower and shave. They couldn't wait.

Once back at the base camp a 2 ½ ton truck pick them up from the helicopter pad and took them to their company area. Roy checked to see which teams were in the field, grabbed a couple of letters from home and headed to his bunk to read them before shaving and taking his shower. Frosty called him over to his hooch and wanted to talk. Frosty told him that he was going to write him up for a valor decoration. Roy laughed and said what for? He told him for the prisoner snatches and the fire fight on our way out. Roy laughed and told him that wasn't worth even talking about. He tried to make light of the whole thing but Frosty was serious. Roy told him if he was going to write him up for some cheap piece of metal then he had to include Larry Styer and the entire team because without them he would not have been able to do what he did. Frosty was insisting that he had to. Roy told him, "Just give me 3 days off." He was leaving the Army and did not want any kind of a label like war hero. He was not and would not accept that label. All he wanted was for his team to get the rewards they deserved. Roy figured that was the end of that but the higher ups had other ideas. He just ignored whatever they said. Acting dumb was easy for him.

On July 15 1968 Sergeant Fred Wheeler led a team on a patrol near Khiem lch. The team included Lt Prescott Smith, James Glaze, Sergeant Hicks, Sergeant Michael Cook, Sergeant Robert Lindley, and five or six PRU's. The purpose of the mission was to discover why the area was so important to the VC. The line companies were receiving heavy fire each time they entered the area.

Once on the ground the team took cover in a heavy wood line. The team froze and listened for a time. After a few minutes the team moved further into the thick jungle, toward a canal. *As* they approached the canal, the team spotted six VC in front of hooch on the opposite bank. The VC were armed, as weapons were visible to the LRRP team. Sergeant Wheeler directed small arms fire across the canal as it wasn't possible to move closer without being spotted by the enemy. During the brief fire fight three bodies fell to the ground.

Hearing movement to their north, the team waited. Because of the kills on the trail, the other members of the enemy unit had left the trail, and were attempting to flank the team's position. However because of the heavy vegetation they encountered after they left the trail, they couldn't move in the team's direction without making one hell of a lot of racket.

The team continued to hear movement to their north and soon realized that the enemy was moving parallel to their position. The enemy seemed to be moving toward the edge of the wood line away from the canal. This meant that they would soon be crossing a wide open rice paddy. Lt Smith radioed for a Light Fire Team helicopters and directed them to the rice paddy.

All of a sudden, an enormous volume of fire erupted from the helicopters overhead and six North Vietnamese Army Regulars, caught in the open rice paddy, were dead. One chopper pilot confirmed, "We caught the bad guys in the open and they didn't have a change."

It wasn't long after "Lantern head" made SP4 that he was given his own team. He ran with one LRRP as the assistant team leader, and five PRUs that were well trained and had plenty of combat experience. His first mission as a team leader would be back to Thoi Son Island. The PBR crew picked up the LRRP team at the Dong Tam dock area well after dark, as this was to be a night insertion. The team was experienced but still had the usual last minute butterflies as the PBR made the last short 30 minute run to the island.

The insertion was made without incident and the team moved quickly to nearby concealment as the PBR backed slowly away from the bank. They would monitor the area for several minutes before moving inland to their objective. As they waited and observed "Lantern head" had thoughts of the day Vaughn was killed. Maybe they could even the score this night.

Seeing that all was clear, the team moved the hundred meters to their objective in the center of the island. There they found a small hooch in the wood line that would provide good concealment. Moving quickly to set up inside the hooch, they encountered an old farmer and his wife who both had the proper identification papers. As the team set up to observe they secured them in their sleeping area. Everything would be quite this night.

The team was instructed to move to the pickup point at first light. The sun was just visible to the east, silhouetting the PBR as the team made their way to the river edge. Encountering no problems, the PBR crew maneuvered to make the pickup. Just as the last LRRP was attempting to get on the boat, they came under automatic rifle fire from a distant tree line.

As team leader, "Lantern head" was the last to board but as he stepped up, his foot slipped and he fell into the water. Thoughts of the last time he was in the water came to his mind as small arms rounds were striking the water all around him. The PBR crew returned fire with the twin .50 caliber machineguns, and the Honeywell (belt fed 40mm grenade launcher) quickly suppressing the enemy fire as the crew pulled "Lantern head" on board.

The PBR crew continued to suppress the fire from the tree line as the LRRP team leader was receiving his Instructions from the TOC at Dong Tam. They were to stay with the PBR while it rearmed then return to the island and bring out a prisoner. By 1400 hours the LRRPs were back on the island, sweeping the area for someone to take back. The enemy had disappeared, but the LRRPs were able to gather several detainees, which they delivered to the MPs at Dong Tam. Thoi Son again proved to be a hostile area to work.

At times the LRRP patrols were misused. An example is a team being used as the point element for an infantry platoon conducting a search and destroy mission. "Lantern head" and five other LRRPs were doing just that when they spotted an old Vietnamese man counting the soldiers. He sent the other five on ahead as he waited for the infantry platoon, informing the Lt. of the old man's activity. Assuming the old man was simply a rice farmer the unit moved on.

Just before night fall they came to a pagoda at the corner of a large rice field. It was bordered on one side by a large canal. Seizing an opportunity to get a good night's rest, the Lt chooses to set his platoon in a defensive position inside the pagoda. He positioned the M-60 machine guns to cover the canal. The infantry platoon was on fifty percent alert so the LRRPs settled in to get as much sleep as they could.

About one in the morning all hell broke loose!! The platoon came under heavy atomic rifle fire and grenade assault. It was a brief, intense attack from what appeared to be an enemy squad of five or six riflemen. The enemy was successful as they wounded three infantrymen, created a fire in the pagoda, and disappeared in to the night. "Lantern head "was sent to recon the area so he and his team low crawled from the pagoda a short distance to a paddy dike. Seeing the enemy squad had departed the area, he informed the Lt that all was clear. Artillery was called in on the suspected route of withdrawal and a sweep of the area was made the following morning.

Sometime in the summer, "Lantern head," J W Boles, Doug MacCullum, and two other LRRPs were the point element for an infantry line company in the Plain Of Reeds. They were conducting a search and destroy mission. The area consisted of very large tall grass (over the head of the average solider) and knee deep water. It was a known infiltration route from Cambodia into the Mekong Delta.

On the fifth day, the LRRPs came across a patch of ground that was above the water table and stretched for a few hundred meters in length and a couple hundred meters wide. There they found a large bunker complex that was unoccupied at the time but showed sign of recent use. They were picked up that afternoon and dropped at a Special Forces camp while the infantry company was taken to a larger area to rest up and get a hot meal. There was quite a lot of excitement at the LRRP Headquarters as they couldn't account for the team for several hours.

After a good night's rest and a hot meal, one platoon from the infantry company was lifted in to destroy the bunker they had found the day before. Unfortunately it turned out to be a disaster waiting to happen. An NVA unit had moved into the area from Cambodia the night prior and surprised the infantry platoon killing all but one.

The LRRP team was inserted with the reinforcing infantry company and under heavy fire going in, Boles was wounded in an attempt to take out a machine gun position. Heavy fighting continued into the afternoon with the Infantry Company taking heavy casualties. Lantern head went to the aid of wounded infantrymen, who had been shot in the head. His helmet was full of blood and as it spilled out onto the ground, his stomach turned. This day continues to haunt him. The NVA were finally forced to retreat under heavy rocket fire and mini guns from the cobra gunships as well as artillery from the nearest US base camp. By the end of the day the infantry company had lost close to two platoons and was evacuated to Dong Tam to regroup.

The LRRPs had a reputation that drew people from all over the division to their company area. Barbecuing steak or chicken was a common occurrence and the beer and soda was always ice cold, compliments of the 1st SGT, Bob "Top" Maushardt. Beer baseball was a memorable event at Dong Tam. Two 55 gallon drums would be filled with beer and ice. The batter would have to drink a beer before he could run to the next base.

Needless to say, the guys were feeling no pain by the third inning or so. It was irrelevant who won. In May or June of 1968, SFC Ray Sonnier stared visiting the area as a guest of "Top".

Sonnier was with the Division G3 and went to Dong Tam with the advance party. In September of 1968 Ray found himself looking for a job as a MSG came into G3 taking his slot. He was slated to go to a SY-OPS unit but while visiting with the LRRP Commander Dale Dickey, and 1ST SGT Bob Maushardt (Sonnier served with Top in Korea) he was offered a spot in the company.

Sonnier's first patrol was with SSG Herbert Dong Cho. The team was compromised early in the patrol and spent the night trying to sleep at a friendly position on a bridge. Someone was constantly throwing grenades in the water and the team got little or no sleep. Ray went out on a few more patrols but due to a hearing profile he was used as a Field 1ST SGT. His main job with the LRRPs was making sure that they got their mail, and keeping them supplied with beer and soda (which was a very difficult job).

SSG Hilan "Jonsey" Jones, SSG Tom Lindly, SSG Jesse Taylor, and SSG Herbert "Frosty" Frost were helping with construction of the TOC Bunker. Jonsey and Frosty came down off the top of the bunker. Sonnier asked them where they thought they were going, and was told by Jonsey that they were hot and needed a beer. Ray told Jonsey that it was not break time, and for them to get back up there. Jonsey smiled at him and very politely told him that he wasn't big enough to make them go back to work. After the beer break everyone returned to the task of roofing the TOC Bunker.

Most of the time, Ray could be found working around the company area and unit club, but on occasions he would go out with a quick reaction team. A team that had been sent out to VC Island called in and said they were in trouble. A quick reaction team was assembled and he went to the supply room get a rifle and ammunition and went out with the team. By the time the reaction team got there the team was near the shore. All the reaction team did was provide them with covering fire while they got on the boat. When Ray attempted to fire his weapon it wouldn't fire. The firing pin had been removed (Jesse Deleon) has never let him forget this).

THE SHIT HOUSE FIRE

BY

ROY BARLEY

Vietnam was a strange place with strange happenings. A real culture shock to see people using oxen to move goods about, living in mudded huts with straw roofs. It felt like we had stepped back in times to the 19th century. After a while we would speak of things like lawns and wonder if they really exist. Simple things, like flush toilets, had become foreign to us. It was a different world than ours and the longer we stayed the more familiar it became. We all looked forward to that "freedom bird", as that was what the flight home was called. Now it was my turn to take the freedom bird flight back to the States. It was the end of September 1968 and the monsoons in IV Corp were just starting.

I was about ready to head back to the world and be discharged at the same time. It was a beautiful sunny day in Vietnam as I went about getting all my clearances to leave. I was turning in my gear at the company supply and generally bullshitting with a couple of friends as we all discussed what we would do back in the world. I'd been thru a year with enough close calls to last me a lifetime. I'd lost a good number of friends on a team I had been a member of. It was a long tough year and I was relieved that I had made it through with no major wounds, as compared to other guys. Sure, caught some shrapnel and such but that was nothing compared to others.

That day was filled with the sounds and smells that went with a war zone. Helicopters coming in and going out; artillery firing in support of men in the field; new guys burning shit, yep that's right: burning shit. Each unit had its own outhouse where the bottom quarter of a 55 gallon steel barrel would slide under the seats. The duty of burning shit, the only way to dispose of it, was usually assigned to new guys in the unit. This happened every day and stirring of the shit was an art that had to be learned. It required a concoction of gas and diesel fuel. 55 gallon barrels close enough to be accessible for starting and continuing the fire without the need of the shit burners to walk too far. It was a job that was unique to Vietnam. This usually went well with no problems; in fact the biggest problem was to insure that you stayed out of the smoke for obvious reasons.

I was standing at the counter of the supply shack when the relative quiet of the day was shattered. A new guy came running in shouting that the shit house was on fire. "The shit house is on fire", "the shit house is on fire", "the shit house is on fire", was all he could say. The expression on his face was that of terror and that was just so funny to me. I mean, how often do you get to hear that expression? I was bent over in laughter when the new guy got serious and told me that it was not funny. All this did was to make me laugh even more. The supply Sgt. handed me a fire extinguisher. I had no idea that we had any of those around. I knew we had lots of C4, ammo; various devices of destruction common to our mission, but I had no idea we had fire extinguishers. Since I had been a member of a volunteer fire company back in the US I had some knowledge of fighting fires so guys looked to me to take charge. So out of the supply shack I went in full run with a fire extinguisher in my hand with others following close behind with more extinguishers. We had a lot more than one extinguisher in the company area, who knew? What would we need those for, except for this occasion. I mean when we were hit with rockets and mortars all they did was explode and kill people but they did not start fires. Back to the shit house fire.

As I left the supply shack I could hear the flames and see the smoke. This was not what I expected. This was a serious fire and the worst sight I saw was the diesel and gas burning as it came out of the faucets on the barrels. The entire side of the shit house was engulfed in flames, but the shit barrels were still burning, and on the outside of the shit house, where they should be. I focused on knocking down the fire burning the fuel coming out and was particularly worried about the gas barrel. I realized that if the gas ran out before the flames were put out there would be one hell of an explosion. I then realized that I could be killed in this fire. I somehow found this funny and started to laugh again. Imagine the letter to my parents: "The President regrets to inform you that your son was killed in a shit house fire." Damn that was funny. We were able to get the flames out in time and got the faucets closed before the gas ran out. The heavy duty leather rappelling gloves we had made it possible to turn the faucets off while still very hot. Now, up pulls a fire truck owned by a private firm (Pacific Engineers and Architects) contracting out to the US. This was not like any fire truck I had ever seen. This was a pickup with a water tank and pump in the back. The truck was staffed with Vietnamese wearing long black rubber rain coats, little helmets and sandals. In fact the rain coats went down to their ankles and really reminded me of a clown car in the circus. The pickup was a small Toyota or Honda. They seemed disappointed that the fire was out but they could use their garden hose to further cool down the fuel barrels. The whole scene was surreal.

When all was said and done I headed to the club for a few beers and some hard stuff. I knew that I had cheated death again. The major question in my mind was what the hell was I was doing with only 2 days left in country. I should have been running the other way. Then again if the fire was not put out in time someone might have been killed or seriously injured. I couldn't live with myself then. I was one day closer to going home and I was still on this side of the dirt.

It was mid December 1968 and the Ranger Company had a couple of teams running missions from fire Support base Moore. Moore was a battalion sized fire base occupied by the 1st Brigade's 24th Battalion, 39th Infantry. The berm was constructed of a dozed perimeter of dirt topped with concertina wire. It was not a fun place to be even during the best of times. The base camp came under frequent mortar and rocket attacks. The mud during the rainy season, and the dust blowing during the dry season, made the living conditions beyond miserable.

Bonding of Warriors

To make matters worse the 2d Battalion S-3 was jacking them around and not providing the support needed while in the field. Captain Dickey thought that if an officer was with the teams that would change, so he sent Lieutenant Prescott (Puck) Smith to insure the proper use and support of the elite ranger teams was implemented.

Just before Lt Smith arrived, one of the LRRP teams lead by Sergeant Ron Wilson came under enemy fire and requested immediate extraction. The call for help was made to the 1st Battalion TOC at Fire Support Base Moore. The assistant, stated that an extraction at night would be too dangerous and the team would have to wait until daylight for extraction. Sergeant "Poncho" Alire, who was the LRRP in the TOC monitoring the transmissions, got in a heated argument with the assistant S-3 and threatened to kick his ass if an extraction helicopter was not sent to get Sergeant Wilson's team immediately.

The new Brigade Commander, Colonel John Geraci was in the command bunker visiting Fire Base Moore, when he heard the transmission and went berserk! (Colonel Geraci had been in the Army for almost thirty years. He had been a Marine Private in WW11, and climbed the battlefield promotion ladder from Private to Master Sergeant as he island hopped through the Pacific. After the war, he went through ROTC training in college to become a lieutenant. He served with distinction in Korea and had since commanded Ranger; Special Forces and Airborne units. In a nutshell, he was one of the greatest combat soldiers who ever stepped into a pair of jungle boots.)

Colonel Geraci fired the assistant S-3 on the spot. He then got on the radio and ordered the immediate extraction of the team. Colonel Geraci, in a fit of rage actually picked the assistant S-3 up and threw him out of the bunker, and then said "Me and the LRRP's are going to Glory." There was no doubt that Colonel Geraci had an uncompromising devotion to the men under his command.

LT Smith arrived at FSB Moore a few days later, finding a completely different attitude toward the LRRPs. He pulled his last mission in country from FSB Moore in the Plain of Reeds, finding the support to be outstanding.

The Shit House Fire

Returning to the States in early January of 1969, Smith was assigned to the Ranger School at Fort Benning. In early May, while working out in the gym on the main post, he ran into Colonel Geraci and was surprised that he remembered him. It was also surprising that Geraci remembered in detail the incident at Fire Base Moore. He was certainly one of the most unforgettable characters that Smith met in Vietnam, or in the Army, for that matter.

Reacting to intelligence provided by a Long Range Patrol, elements of the 2d Battalion, 39th Infantry and gunships of the 3d Squadron 17th Air Cavalry killed 86 Viet Cong on November 30th. It was the second time in a week that the Brigade "Recondos" had capitalized on air cavalry firepower and surveillance to post a large body count.

The Long Range Patrol sighted the enemy force between Cal Lay and Cai Be the night of 29 November. Early the next morning, Troop A of the 3d/17th scouted the area and found the VC near where they had been seen previously. Within an hour, Company D of the 2d/39th had air-mobled to the west of the enemy and company A to the northeast. Moving through open areas covered with small, muddy streams, the 9th Division soldiers swept toward a Nipa palm and banana tree line. As the infantry pressed in from two sides, artillery pounded at each end of the VC position and the gunships sought out individuals and small groups of enemy soldiers. Each element protected the others as they closed in on the VC.

After the final count, gunships had killed 52 enemy soldiers, and accounted for 16 weapons captured. Company D killed 26 VC and captured 13 weapons, while Company A killed eight and took four weapons. Nine suspects were detained and one VC rallied to the Open Arms program during the day long operation. The only U.S. casualty was one man wounded.

"This was not a typical Delta operation," said Captain Bob Stephens of Cherry Hill, New Jersey, assistant brigade officer. "We usually have to dig them out of the bunkers and the Nipa palm, but this was a turkey shoot. The air cav caught over 40 of them moving in the open in broad day light."

Christmas Eve day started out like any other at Tan An, except there was supposedly a cease fire in effect for the holiday. Most of the guys had been through "TET" and knew what a cease fire was all about. 10 A.M. rolled around and Duane "Poncho" Alire told everyone to be at the chopper pad by 4 P.M. as they would be going to Dong Tam for the Bob Hope Christmas Show. Everyone got all gussied up and loaded their libations to take along for the Christmas party at Dong Tam.

They arrived at the pad about 4 P.M. Dan Bien looked around and saw Jimmy "old man" Booth, Ronald Kneer, Michael "Cookie" Cook, Bob Pegram, Richard "Richie" Bellwood (who was just back from the hospital from a shrapnel wound to his neck on one of Weber's missions). Ronald Weber, Jim Thayer, Garth Volbright, Jesse DeLeon, and a few others. 5 P.M. came and went and no ride. 6 P.M. still no ride. Jimmy popped open his jug of VO and started to make bubbles! It was almost dark when the chopper finally arrived. Dan was careful boarding as he had a jug of VO in each side pocket of his trousers.

Vietnam at dusk was a beautiful sight from a chopper. It was just a short hop to Dong Tam and as they un-assed the chopper Dan went around to the window and offered the pilots a jug. They thought he was offering a drink and refused as they were flying. The pilot finally opened the window and Dan shoved in a full bottle and wished him a Merry Christmas. He smiled and returned the Christmas wish.

The guys walked the couple of blocks from the flight line to the company area arriving at the club to find it full of guys they hadn't seen in ages. This turned out to be better than any high school reunion could ever be. The brewskies and war stories flowed with many an "I can top that one" as the group celebrated. They were keeping an eye out for Cook's team which was coming in from My Phouc Tay. The rest of the guys from Tan An got there but there was no sign of the group from My Phouc Tay. Word came that they couldn't get a chopper in that late to pick up the team so the party continued without them.

About 11: P.M. Duane and Dan were well on their way and decided that since this was Christmas Eve what better way to celebrate than with some red and green star clusters, with a few white ones thrown in for good measure. Off they went to the ammo connex. Dan with his trusty zippo in hand providing light as he searched among the C-4, composition B, hand grenades, and all types of assorted ammunition, for the sought after flares. He finally found the star clusters and started pitching them out to Poncho who finally yelled out that they had enough. Now, where to launch them from? It was decided that the top of the T.O.C. bunker would suit the need just right.

Once on top of the bunker the countdown began, 5 minus 4...... Dan popped a red one while Poncho popped a green one, then a white, green, a red and so on. Sirens started to go off so they ducked down thinking the base was under mortar attack. A short while later a jeep screamed up the road and stopped in front of the T.O.C. There was a bunch of screaming. The company C.Q. was yelling too. Whoever it was they got back in the jeep, pulled up to the corner and was heading away when Dan popped a white cluster just above his windshield. After that things blurred.

The next thing Dan remembered was being cold and wet. He was awakened to incessant quacking around his head. About that time he opened his eyes and heard someone say "hey Sarge you better get cleaned up, Ernie Banks will be here in about an hour." There he was, in the ditch, alongside of the road with the ducks. He got out and cleaned up, then headed over to the bleachers to meet the rest of the guys. Sure enough here comes Ernie Banks. Dan couldn't believe his eyes.

"Ernie," "What the hell you doing here in Vietnam?" He asked. He said it was the off season and thought it was a good idea to come over and help boost the troop's morale. Dan had to pinch himself. Being from the Chicago area, Ernie left with one of his trademark slogans, "The Cubs will shine in 69." There was time for lunch before heading over to the show. The place was packed. Dan doesn't remember who opened but Bob Hope finally came out on stage. There was an air strike on VC Island. After the first bomb hit, Bob crouched down, then jumped up looking over the back of the stage at the big black cloud and remarked, "What the hell was that?" Someone yelled out, "That's "War" Bob!"

Ann Margret came on stage and did she ever look bad, like 1,000 miles of bad road, but she finally came around toward the end of her

BONDING OF WARRIORS

set. All in all the guys felt lucky to have seen the show before hiking back to the company area for the ride back to Tan An.

Someone inquired how the guys were to get back to Tan An before Christmas dinner (one just like home) was served. They were told that someone would take them back in a "duce and a half." Loading up with some F.N.G. driving and another one riding shot gun and it was off to Tan An. The bone jarring shifting caused someone to ask the driver if he had a driver's license. He mumbled something none of the Rangers could hear. As they headed out of the gate from Dong Tam a couple of them stood up and rode leaning on the cab of the truck. The breeze felt good.

You can remember Highway 4 as being two paved lanes with a short shoulder and a 6' to 8' drop off to the rice paddies below. Well, they were progressing nicely when up ahead loomed a column of trucks stopped for some reason or another. It appeared to be an ARVN convoy. Dan yelled down for the driver to slow down.

He will never forget the three ARVN soldiers, squatting in the shade at the back of the last truck, eating something from their bowls with chopsticks. The load of Rangers was bearing down on them at neck breaking speed. The driver yelled that he had no breaks. Someone yelled for him to downshift to reduce the speed. You could see the terror in the eyes of the ARVN soldiers as the "duce & a half" bore down on them. They finally dove head long into the rice paddy. As contact was made, the sound of bumper meeting bumper echoed ahead. The ARVN's were not happy campers. Finally someone said "Back this thing up and let's get out of here." As they passed the convoy they met stares that were not friendly at all. Somehow they made it to Tan An in time for Christmas dinner and received a "ditty bag" from the Donut Dollies. What a Christmas it had been.

GENERAL EWELL'S LAUNDRY

BY

DAN BIEN

Don't even ask me how or why, but while at Dong Tam, sometime in December, I went to mama-sans laundry to pick up some of my clothes. After I got back to the hooch I opened up the freshly starched uniforms and started putting them away when I made the big discovery. There was the fully embroidered shirt of the 9th Division's Commanding General, two star Julian J. Ewell, right there in front of me. What was I going to do? I found Poncho and Counts. They looked at it and said "Hey, let's put it on and take pictures. We can send them home and say we made it to the Big Time." Little Jonsey and a couple of others showed up and wanted their pictures taken wearing the shirt as well.

After our photo session I locked it up in my footlocker. After supper Poncho said that he was going to head up to the Donut Dollies compound for a visit and wanted me to come along, but I had letters to write and begged off.

About an hour or so later the C.Q. came and got me. He said someone wanted to talk to me on the berm. It was Poncho. He said lets have some fun with the shirt. I asked "how?" He said wear it over to the Donut Dollies compound. I told him he was out of his mind and he prodded me on. Finally I agreed. I put the shirt on knowing full well I was going to L.B.J. (Long Binh Jail) for impersonating an officer.

My route took me right through the headquarters area. I was glad it was dark. Someone approached me from the opposite direction and I was glad that the area was dimly lit. We passed but I wasn't recognized. When I got to the compound the place was surrounded by M.P.s. As I walked up to the gate one of them snapped to attention and saluted. I thought for sure I was in deep trouble. I returned the salute and the M.P. said "Evening Sir". I told him to "Carry on" as I walked up to the door of the compound. As I opened the door and stepped inside someone shouted "Attention" and everyone got to their feet and saluted. They looked and saw that I was not General Ewell. The salute fell and I knew my goose was cooked. Everybody started to laugh and I felt better. Our company commander, Dale Dickey, was in attendance as well as other captains, majors, and colonels. To my everlasting relief somebody said "Let me have that shirt. I want to have fun with it." I was glad to relinquish the shirt as I had all the fun I had ever wanted with it. I was looking for Poncho as I fully wanted to strangle him right there in front of his beloved Donut Dollies.

Dan was not superstitious but when word came alerting them for a mission by PBR out of Tan An that night he had second thoughts. "Poncho" came with the operations order and they headed for the docks on the beautiful Van Co Tay River. The team was to head up river along the Plain Of Reeds almost to Moc Hoe, a stone's throw from Cambodia. The mission would be to monitor for any sampan traffic.

Meeting the captain of the lead PBR they went over the plan. The captain pointed on the map to where there was a cut at the narrow end of an ox-bow. He explained they had been ambushed there a couple of nights before. They would take the same route that night. Dan told the boat captain that he was short with only thirteen days to go. The captain commented that he wasn't superstitious. That made him feel better!!

At dusk they headed up river toward the destination. Just as the boats entered the ox-bow short cut, they drew fire from the south bank. Making it out of the kill zone the boats regrouped a mile or so up river to check for casualties and damage. It was a wonder that no one was hit and the boats survived. Up ahead there was a confrontation going on with gunships and flares that lit up the night sky right where the patrol was to go.

The mission was aborted and gunships were called to cover the exit out of the ambush area. None were available. The boats would have to make it out on their own. Knowing about where the ambush had occurred, they would be ready. All available firepower was lined up along the gunwale. The Rangers were ready with their rifles as well as the Navy's machine gunners on both boats. The boat captain told his crew "Let's go," and off they went. When the lead boat hit the area he opened up with all he had and was followed in short order by those on the trailing boat. Dan didn't recall receiving fire at that time.

Making it back to Tan An in the wee hours of the morning the patrol leader called for a vehicle to pick them up. The roads hadn't been cleared so if the guys wanted to get back to camp they would have to walk. Anxious to return and get some sleep they opt to walk the short distance home. As they crossed the bridge over the river the rangers found the G.I.'s guarding the approach asleep. They were tempted to take the machine gun but decided to wake them instead. As they neared the gate one of the guards hollered "Halt." "Who goes there?" They were tired, upset, and anxious to get some sleep. They were not in the mood to play games. Needless to say, they let them in.

Dan went straight to the Tactical Operations Center and was greeted by an "S-2" major who exclaimed. "Oh, by the way, you were ambushed by Charlie Company 2nd of the 60th." When Dan heard that they had been ambushed by friendly fire he went off to the tune of "With all due respect Sir, if we could have gotten gunships to cover our ass as we broke out of the area you'd be writing a hundred or so letters to those guys, folks," and walked out.

It wasn't that the route hadn't been cleared to insure that there were no friendly troops in the area. The Rangers were told that they were in "Charlie Country," which seemed to account for the confusion. Dan is bothered to this day of the ramifications if they would have gotten the gunships. He shudders at the thought.

"Poncho" came in with the operations order for Ron Weber's next mission. Bob Pegram and Dan Bien were scheduled for radio relay. They would set up with Bravo Company 2nd of the 60th at Thu Thua (too-a-too-a.) Unfortunately their transportation broke down. As they waited for the jeep to be fixed they wondered if they would get set up in time. Once it was fixed they made it to Thu Thua just in time to set up the 292 antennas and radio, then have a "hot pack" supper prior to the team's insertion.

The night passed unevenly, but as Bob and Dan surveyed the surroundings. They were both glad that they didn't end up in an outfit like that. The trip back to Tan An was also uneventful. They would make one more journey to Thu Thua before heading back to Dong Tam.

With four days to go, Duane got word to head back to Dong Tam to get ready to DEROS. The next day, Dan finally got word to head back as well. Arriving at Dong Tam, Dan found that Jim Counts, and Richard Jones had not received their orders. The next day (two days to go) his orders were cut and he started to clear out. He was given the usual re-up talk and really thought about it. Bob Pegram, Gary Beckham, Jim Counts, and Richard "Little Jonesy," Jones decided they would extend the 45 days and get out for good. Poncho had opted to go home. Dan thought about it as he looked around at all the new people who had arrived in recent weeks and felt like he should stay to help out.

Headed for the "club" Dan ran into Richard Bellwood. He stopped him asking, "Richie, whose going to keep an eye on you when I leave?" Bellwood replied "Don't worry Sergeant Bien. I can take care of myself." Wondering out loud if he really meant that, Bellwood assured him that he would make it okay. That helped Dan make up his mind. He let LT Dickey know of his intentions. Dan would later suffer great remorse over his decision when informed by letter from Pegram of Richards demise along with a bunch of others.

Poncho and Dan loaded up their gear in a 2 ton and were given a ride to Bien Hoa for the appointment with a "Freedom Bird" and a trip across the pond to a place called home. Words cannot express the torture of the last 24 hours in-country as you waited for your name to be called at "Port Call." When it finally comes you are too exhausted to fully comprehend the joyful feeling of going home. After boarding the plane and taxing down the runway, no one drew a breath until the plane reached an altitude that they all felt safe from being shot down. "What a long strange trip it had been!"

DELTA RANGER EMPLOY CHARLIES TACTICS

BY

JACK BICK

Jack Bick was an Army combat journalist and photographer that often participated in Ranger operations. He wrote for the "Stars and Stripes" which was a daily publication, and the "Old Reliable", which was a weekly publication. The following is one of his articles written and published in the "Old Reliable" that describes some of the E Company Ranger Tactics used in the Mekong Delta.

Tan An, South Vietnam, 1969--Six men wait patiently on the bank of the Bo Bo Canal late one night on the edge of the Plain of reeds. They were dressed in battle gear including camouflaged fatigues and stick makeup.

A sampan approached from the south but came into shore below their position. The three men in the boat had AK-47s and two of them began to circle the American position. Meanwhile another sampan approached from the south.

The Americans calmly waited for the second sampan to enter their kill zone before opening up with automatic weapons fire killing four occupants. Without hesitation they swung around to kill the circling two enemy combatants as the man guarding the first sampan escaped into the thick nipapalm.

"They wore black and khaki clothing and carried AK-47s," said Sergeant John A. Faracco, Long Island, NY. "They were very possibly NVA."

The ambushers were team 14, part of Company E, 75th Infantry (Rangers), attached to the 3rd Brigade, 9th Infantry Division. These special groups of men have a big bag of tricks to employ against the Viet Cong. All tactics are offensive operations rather than long range reconnaissance patrols employed by the other ranger teams in Vietnam. The tactics are especially suited to small Ranger teams, as well as the swampy Mekong Delta area of operations.

"In the Delta terrain the recon mission is not practical," said company commander, First Lieutenant Albert C. Zapanta, Monterey Park, CA. "Because of the flat, open landscape, a team would compromise its position within 48 hours or less and the watery paddies would cause wrinkled skin and emersion foot."

They turned to offensive combat tactics including six mission types; the overnight ambush, the raid, the "parakeet" flight, the 12 or 18-man hunter-killer, the stay behind and the daylight mission. These are in order of most use. All can be executed as preplanned operations or as flash missions with as little as 15 minutes from notification to an awaiting chopper.

Major General Harris W. Hollis, last commanding general of the 9th Division in Vietnam highly recommended the company for Valorous Unit Award by writing, "The men displayed extraordinary heroism as they frequently engaged enemy forces superior in numbers to their unit. Relying on the element of surprise and their often superior fire power, the men distinguished themselves time and again by their selfless and unrelenting offensive pressure on the enemy."

Every mission begins with an intelligence report. "Each day we have confidential sources of intelligence info," said Staff Sergeant Timothy R. Oschwald, MI. "Previous reports are then checked for a pattern of enemy movement plus friendly operations in that area."

From the intelligence, four areas of operations are picked and cleared through brigade headquarters. Assets are scheduled for insertion and support in the field. Team Leaders are briefed on their objective, the intelligence report, and American activity and their assets. Some areas of operation, when possible, are visually re-conned from the air by two team members a few hours before insertion.

"Basically we are looking for a point for insertion, enemy activity, a good ambush position and a defensive position," said team leader Sergeant Bob Wallace, Barnard, KS.

Fire power is important to a small team and therefore at least one man, possible two, carry an "over and under" M-79 grenade launcher mounted under an M-16 with a modified hand grenade. Other members carry straight M-16s.

THE OVERNIGHT AMBUSH

The overnight ambush requires this type of concentrated fire power. Team 21 has been most successful with the overnight mission. Operating Aug. 10, 1969 in the Plain of Reeds on the Bo Canal, they killed six NVA soldiers moving south. Immediately after the ambush, the team members waded into the canal to recover the cargo from the two sampans. They came up with 66 B-40 rockets, five 107mm rockets, and an AK-47 and personal military equipment. This weaponry would not be deployed against us.

"They had no idea we were there," said Staff Sergeant Jim Koening, Richmond, VA. "One got his rifle up but was hit before he could return against our concentrated fire."

THE RAID

Eleven days later, the same team entered an area 20 miles southwest of Saigon, reported by intelligence sources to hold a main hospital for VC and NVA patients.

Before they could set up, the Rangers initiated contact with three armed enemy and while searching for the bodies, they uncovered a hooch hidden under an overgrowth of vines. Further searching uncovered other

Bonding of Warriors

hoochs and tunnels containing medical supplies, surgical equipment, hammocks, clothing, food and bedding for up to 40 patients plus escape tunnels. Documents included a list of VC and NVA causalities.

The complex was not completely searched until morning. During the night Team 27 was inserted by boat as reinforcement. As enemy movement around the position increased, a 33-man volunteer Ranger reaction team was inserted by air to hold the position. Six enemies were killed during the night, one by a "Spooky: gunship, two by the Rangers and three by Navy Sea Wolf helicopter gunships

"My team was in there two times before and spotted movement," said team leader, Staff Sergeant Paul A. Newman, Mentor Lake, OH. "This time we made contact in what turned out to be the perimeter of the hospital we knew was in the area."

Rangers like to use the enemy's own tactics and the raid is designed to do specifically that. Using a preplanned insertion point, they use surprise to put the enemy off balance.

One of the most successful raids involved Team 11 and resulted in 13 enemy dead. The Rangers landed in a very small paddy completely surrounded by nipapalm tree lines.

"Our PRU (People's Recon Unit) killed one before we were even off the chopper," said Sergeant Michael Glowinski, Courtland, NY. Another was killed as the Rangers moved into a hooch area and saw him gathering up AK-47 rifles. "They were so surprised that some of the dead were still sitting at tables," said Glowinski.

THE PARAKEET

Closely related is the "Parakeet" flight. One of the men said of it: "This is what Charlie would do if he had choppers."

The "parakeet" is much like the raid except that the insertion point is not specific. A "slick" helicopter with six Rangers flies a low level visual recon supported by a light fire team, a light observation helicopter and a cobra gunship. They look for a target of opportunity and immediately insert upon sighting anything suspicious.

"Basically we charge an area suspected of housing VC," said Sergeant Anthony Mosley, Honolulu, HI. "If the enemy is there and runs, we cut him down. If he stays to fight, we break into teams and maneuver."

One such "parakeet" mission accounted for seven enemy dead plus a bonus of a 60mm mortar tube and three rounds found inside a hooch.

The hooch, with military equipment on the ground outside, caught the alert eye of one Team 22 Ranger. They immediately inserted only 25 meters from the hooch. The VC were cooking breakfast but reacted fast enough to return fire.

Supported by gunships, the fire fight lasted about five minutes. The Rangers killed three and the gunships four. One killed by the gunships was found some distance away after another insertion and was suspected to be the mortar officer.

THE HUNTER-KILLER

The largest unit that the Rangers work with is the 12 or 18-man hunter-killer team. The mission is to find contact and sustain it until the enemy is defeated. The technique is to use one team as the hunter to find contact with the enemy, the other team maneuvers to the flanks for the kill. Many times the M-60 is part of the equipment because fire superiority is very important in this type of tactic.

The hunter team usually probes a wood line while the killer element waits in the rice paddy. It is important for the waiting team to be alert and quiet. "When I watch a tree line," said Specialist Four Steve Wells, Port Arthur, TX, "I get to know every tree and leaf. If anything changes or moves, I'll know it."

In the first three missions in Kien Hoa Province, the hunter-killer technique accounted for 14 enemy dead.

THE STAY BEHIND

The hunter-killer tricks the enemy into believing there are only a small number of Americans in the area. The "stay behind" is designed to make the enemy believe there are no Americans remaining in the area.

"We inserted on choppers that were extracting an infantry company," said the leader of team 17, Sergeant Wes Watson, Twin Falls, IA. The enemy didn't have any idea that the Rangers were in the area as six armed VC came into the paddy talking and laughing. "They were probably going to see if anything useful was left behind and were caught completely unaware," said Watson. Four of the six were killed outright while the other two left blood trails to a nearby canal where they probably drowned.

DAYLIGHT MISSION

One of the most significant victories for the Rangers over the enemy was on August 24 1969 when they were on a flash daylight mission and killed the highest ranking Viet Cong in Long An Province.

"Stogie helicopters of the 3rd Squadron, 17th Air Cavalry spotted sleeping positions and received a B-40 rocket and AK fire. The Rangers were called and ten men of Teams 11 and 14 inserted a short time later. Three enemy were lying in the waist high grass and ankle deep water. One tried to throw a grenade but was killed before he could pull the pin. Another was killed a short distance away. Continuing a sweep of the area, the Rangers came upon the third VC who surrendered. "Stogie" killed three more who tried to flee from the men on the ground.

The "Hoi chanh" also identified one of the dead as Colonel Hai Tram, commander of an enemy area of operations that encompassed most of Long An Province. Personal records found on his body indicated that he had been working for the Communists since 1935. He and his party were on their way to Cambodia for a rest.

"The Rangers have a great deal of flexibility in tactical operations as pictured by the brigade," said 3d Brigade commander, Colonel Dale J.

Crittenger, Washington DC. "They have self-confidence and individual capability and therefore we are able to commit them as a small team on selective targets.

Individual capability comes from training. Many of the men are Recondo School qualified and some have participated in the 9th Division Sniper program. Though training, the men of Company E, 75th Infantry learn how to effectively fight a guerrilla war.

Training coupled with each success leads to self-confidence. This self-confidence builds the spirit that is a distinguishing characteristic of the unit. It is not uncommon to see these men volunteer for a mission even when they are off the line and have taken a rear echelon job within the company.

"This unit is composed of select men," said Sergeant Ray P. Davis, San Diego, Ca. "Every man is dependable, which is a must when working in small groups and using Charlie's own tactics. I'm proud to have been chosen for this unit."

"1969"

COMPILED BY

BILL CHEEK

I carried 3 M-14 pouches and 1 canteen on my web belt. The M-14 pouches could hold 5 M-16 magazines. We put a piece of black electrical tape on the butt of each magazine to form a tab so that we could pull the first 4 magazines out of the pouch easier and then we sliced the top half inch or so of the pouches that so we could lay the 5th magazine across the top. I generally liked to carry 2 of these pouches loaded with tracers every 3rd round and the other pouch had all ball rounds for penetrating heavy growth or for firing without giving my location away so easily. I also liked to carry 2 magazines in my leg pockets loaded with straight tracers, just for marking my or the enemy's location for the fly boys when the radio could not do the job accurately enough for me. I also had 2 magazines taped together in a V shape in my weapon for quick reaction reloading at first contact. In the really bad areas, I also carried 1 or more 7 magazine bandoleers made of OD cloth and from 6 to 15 grenades of various types and a claymore as well as the PRC-25. Needless to say, when the mud got thick, I was walking deep. Almost forgot the big starlight scope also!

The following mission explains why I was not a fan of all tracer loads. One night in January of 1969, Herb Frost, Roman Mason, Leon Moore, Mark Durham and I were on a mission east of Ben Tre in a populated area with much tree growth separated by small rice paddies and Vietnamese hooch's every hundred meters or so. We were moving from hooch to hooch looking for military age males or any sign of weapons when we spotted a man walking at us from a wooded area. When he was about half way across the rice paddy, we called to him to stop. He took off like a ruptured duck and managed to dodge our fire. That SOB could have been an Olympic champion sprinter.

About 45 minutes later a bunch of his friends came into the area to return our greeting. We were in a hooch searching for weapons when a large volume of fire went over the roof. The local VC seemed to know there were 2 women and a small kid in the hooch with us so avoided shooting directly into the place. This gave us a definite advantage. I was on one corner and had cut a slit through the thatched wall just above a mud wall and could see the VC firing positions every time they popped up to shoot. There was enough star light and a few clicks away someone was shooting illumination rounds that partially backlit their position. One of them must have been a FNG VC because he was shooting almost all tracers and each time he popped up to shoot, he cut loose with all 30 rounds just over my head but still above the roof. Keep in mind that this was not a heavy battle but, rather, just friendly exchanges of lead to let each of us know that the other guy was there.

I saw this guy pop up twice from the same spot and empty his magazine, so I was waiting; when he did it for the 3rd and final time. As soon as I saw his solid line of green tracers start, I was aimed in at that spot and cut loose with a clip of mixed ball and tracer. I bet 3/4th of my load caught him in the upper chest and face. I watched as his tracer line climbed into the sky before stopping. At that point, the other VC reduced fire and quit using tracers.

A few minutes later they must have decided they had enough of us and pulled their X-FNG off for last rites. We decided that it was time to go, so we called for extraction. I remember wondering if any had stayed behind to give us a going away party when the bird came, but if so, they did no more shooting as we pulled out. Tracers were a nice tool but they work in both directions. This also shows the kind of problems we had in the delta with LRRP missions. There was way too much population and too little solid cover in many areas.

Bonding of Warriors

Trapped in a mud-walled hooch by a superior VC force 29 years ago one of my team scouts went to sleep on rear security ....on a night when 60 or more very unfriendly people were out searching for us in at least 3 groups. Unfortunately, one of their elements found us from that direction first and damn near bagged our whole team. Below is the story of that night. An earlier version of it was published in "Behind Enemy Lines "magazine in 1993. For any of you active duty guys, please kick the shit out of anyone you ever find asleep on guard duty. It might help save the lives of them and others.

On 25 January 1969, a long range reconnaissance patrol in Dinh Tuong Province came under an intense barrage of hostile fire from a numerically superior force. As the patrol neared a wood line, they were completely exposed and came under a murderous hail of fire. Specialist Bellwood courageously engaged the enemy with his rifle, quickly silencing two of the nearest hostile emplacements, giving his comrades time to reach cover. As he continued to lay down heavy base of suppressive fire, he was mortally wounded by an enemy round.

A LRRP team fights for survival. With half the team KIA and the team leader blinded, gunships, and medevac are the survivors only hope.

January 27, 1969 started out just like many other for Team 17. Sergeant Rick Ehrler was the Team leader and was preparing for yet another night ambush patrol off the Mobile Riverine Force. He served with E/50 Long Range Patrol from April 68 through January 69. We had teams scattered all over the 9th Division AO. Several months earlier, our teams were kicked off the Mobile Riverine Force for smuggling beer on board. Shortly thereafter a VC sapper team swam out to the USS Westchester County near Thoi Son Island with a large quantity of plastic explosives and blew two large holes in it. We were quickly forgiven and invited to return to the ship. We began running ambush patrols along trails and canals within a few klicks of the MRF. In the previous three weeks, we had pulled several effective missions on the south bank area near a major swamps canal intersection called the "cross roads." This area was roughly between My Tho and Ben Tre and consisted of large sections of heavy forest and jungle swamps boarder by kilometers of wide open rice paddies. About half of those missions resulted in contact with a very active local VC force.

On this mission, I planned to insert by chopper near a heavy wood line and move the team several hundred meters to a position near one of the canals. Late on that afternoon, I flew over the area in a LOH to pick out some possible sites while on the way to drop off George Calabrese and Chuck Semmit at Ben Tre to be our radio relay. Shortly after returning to the MRF, the Huey arrived and carried six of us off into what turned out to be deep shit.

At our first insertion point, we were only on the ground about thirty seconds before a VC strolled out of the woods a hundred meters away with his AK over his shoulder like a hobo's pack. He spotted me and jumped back into the woods just as I cut loose with a burst from my 16. I decided at that point to extract and move a couple clicks to see if we could get a clean insertion. We landed near a small hooch I remembered from a previous mission to be a water buffalo shed. It was almost dark as I scanned the wood line. At that point, I decided it was going to be an interesting night, because there was a Vietnamese man in the woods looking right back at me. When I reported this, I was told we were to keep the mission going anyway. I waited until full dark and got the team moving out of there. About an hour later, I heard a brief burst of fire from the vicinity of our last position. Figured that we had escaped unseen, but we were not able to get into the woods because of heavy movement of people on their way home. We came to a cluster of five hoochs scattered over an area the size of a football field. All but one appeared to be empty. We entered one that was isolated from the others and found it to be built like a fortress. It had thick mud walls, about four feet high, which ran all the way around except for the door opening and a large above-ground bunker of mud and tree trunks. Because of a dry thatch wall on one side, which would have caused too much noise to remove, I had to deploy two men outside on the corner. This should have caused no problem, as they could quickly jump over the wall and knock holes in the thatching if it became necessary. For the next several hours we waited and watched to see what would happen.

BONDING OF WARRIORS

At 2300 hours, I put the team on 50% alert. Richard Thompson, Mark Durham, and Roman Mason took their shot at getting some sleep, Norman Crabb, Leon Moore and I watched for any activity. Around 2320 hours I thought I saw movement in the woods about 150 meters away. It was a clear night with starlight so bright I could almost read by it. I moved to Moore's position to use the starlight scope. He said there had been no activity on his side of the hooch, away from the wood line. For the next few minutes, Norman Crab and I observed what appeared to be about twenty people moving around in the woods across from us. I was not overly concerned, because I had claymores set up in that direction.

Just as I decide to wake the team for possible action and to contact base, I heard voices behind me. Thinking it was Mason and Moore, I grabbed my 16 and started around the hooch to shut them up and get them inside. I had just turned the corner of the hooch when I recognized the voices were Vietnamese, and five armed VC stood four feet from me. They were so preoccupied looking down at the sleeping forms of my rear security element they did not even notice me. I raised my 16 to waste them when I noticed about twenty more VC on the other side of a paddy dike ten feet past Mason and Moore's position. I slipped back around the corner and had Crabb cover the closest VC while I moved inside to wake the other guys. I looked over the wall as I whispered into the radio for assistance. We were unable to figure a sure way to wake Mason and Moore and get them in before they would be hit. There must have been at least twenty weapons trained on them at point blank range. My radio relay people told me that division would not send gunships until we were in contact. I told everyone to open up at once, hoping that we could put out enough fire to allow Mason and Moore to get inside. It did not work, and they were cut down before they could even start to move.

The mud walls of the hooch held up against the heavy battering from all those AK's and the thick roof thatching absorbed the blast from several grenades. So far, the people I spotted in the wood line had not started firing. I figured they wanted us to run from the hooch into their ambush, but I was not about to leave Mason and Moore behind, even if I could. I decided to remove my radio and crawl around the hooch to a point where I could fire along the right flank of the attacking force, when I spotted more people on my left flank. We were completely surrounded and taking fire from three sides. About that time, an RPG came in the door and detonated on the ground three feet in front of me. I think the blast caused me to do a complete back flip while flying about fifteen feet across the hooch. For the first few seconds, it felt like someone hit me in the face with a two by four, but it quickly numbed into a dull throb. I could not see anything, even though there had been enough light in the hooch before from tracers to see quite well.

I crawled back across the floor, feeling for my 16 and the radio, when I heard another large blast to my right. Thompson fell to the floor and died almost immediately. Only about five minutes had passed since the first shot, and half my team was KIA, and I was blind. I found my 16 and asked my radio relay team where the Cobras were. I was told they were on the way and Hotel-Volley 27, the call sign of a 105 battery at fire base Claw came up on my frequency and asked if we wanted artillery support. With VC within 10 to 20 feet away and me blind, I said no. I could not pull one of my last two men off the wall long enough to call in 105's on our own heads.

After about fifteen minutes of heavy firing, Crabb came to me to say he was out of ammo and Durham was on his last magazine. Since I had been blinded so early in the fight, I had plenty left. I started handing magazines to them and then finally handed my web gear to Crabb after removing a grenade to keep just in case we were overrun. I noticed that the VC fire was also slacking off and figured they were also running low. I told Crabb and Durham to start shooting semi-automatic at selective targets to keep us going as long as possible. I called once again to ask where the hell our gunships were and to advise that in a few more minutes they would only need to send graves registration for a reaction force. One of the sweetest sounds I can remember hearing was when Charger 21 told me to mark my position so his gun ships could open up. I had Crabb throw my strobe light out the door and said anything more than twenty feet from it was all theirs. The VC that could, hauled ass out of there as rockets and mini-guns started tearing up the area. I told Crabb and Durham that we would drag out the dead teammates when the extraction ship landed, and if there was no effective sniper fire they could go back for our equipment. A chopper crew with balls like King Kong landed in that mess and waited on the ground for us to load. Crabb led me to the bird to keep me from walking into the tail rotor. The gunships did such a great job of building a wall of lead and fire that we had no problem extracting.

I spent the next ten and a half months recovering from wounds and learning how to live as a blind man. Well it could have been a whole hell of a lot worse. I recently got back in touch with some of the old gang and it is great. My times at the Ranger reunions and at the Wall have been a terrific way to heal the old wounds.

On occasion a LRRP team will get lucky and find something big. That was the case on 25 January when a team led by Michael O' Day exposed an NVA company: called in gunships were extracted, and turned the action over to the 3rd Brigade. A text book mission, one of many, conducted by the LRRPs.

At dusk on 26 February 1969, the "Hunter Killer "team was inserted into an LZ in an open rice paddy by two Huey slicks, escorted by a pair of gunships. It was a cold LZ.

David Stone was point man and the team leader for the "Hunter Killer" team. On landing, Stone noticed many places on and around the LZ where the reeds were bent over as if someone had recently been sitting on them. He reckoned a large enemy force had just vacated the area because the reeds were bending back as he watched.

Most likely, it was a large infiltrating enemy force coming out of Cambodia with orders not to get decisively engaged, who were taking ten when they saw the insertion birds, realizing trouble was on its way and hightailed it into the woods. Something gave Stone an uneasy feeling. The terrain did not jive with the map and the matted down grass bothered him.

Stone was a veteran Ranger leader. It was probably his sixth sense, developed during dozens of such missions, shouting: "danger, danger, danger." He quickly moved the force off the LZ and into the nearby woods. Stopping when they came to a clearing. He then wisely called for a marking round to check his position, in case he was in the middle of a large enemy force, he'd be able to bring in the artillery big stick. Just at that moment, Sergeant Wesley Watson, who was at the rear of the column, saw an enemy soldier dressed in Khakis about 15 meters from him. Before he could get a shot off the guy disappeared into the darkness. Then a single shot was heard.

Not knowing what was going on in the rear of his column, he relished that the team had lost "surprise" when the signal shot was heard, and trouble was on the way. He set his forces up in a tight perimeter and waited for the artillery marking round. Suddenly four dinks walked into the clearing. A Ranger yelled "La Dai" and when they ran, they joined the ranks of the KIA.

Sergeant Stone threw a grenade. It hadn't gone more than a foot when an explosion went off behind him, and blew him out of the wood line and into the clearing. He was hit in the back by shrapnel and momentarily stunned, his shocked brain trying to connect his grenade with the explosion that came from the opposite direction. Then more explosions clobbered the perimeter as incoming M-79 rounds, hand grenades and B-40 rockets were fired at the Ranger position. The common quote from all survivors was "all hell broke loose."

Thirty-two years after the saga, Ranger Wesley Watson said the minute the team landed a VC watching the LZ spotted them. "A few minutes later we started talking heavy arms fire. We returned fire and that brought a barrage of RPG fire aimed at the trees above us, creating air burst, which what is caused so many casualties so quickly."

The Rangers blasted back with three M-60 machine guns, an XM-203 Over and Under-combined M16 and M79-- and a dozen M16s. The intensity of the Ranger return fire probably stopped an enemy attack as they must've realized they didn't have some small LRRP team-- they had a tiger by the tail, a heavily armed "Hunter Killer Force!"

The enemy backed off fast. Even though Sergeants Stone and Charles Chester were both hit they worked on the other wounded Rangers. Ranger Warren Lizotte was seriously wounded in the head exposing part of his brain. Sergeant Stone tended to him while Chester patched up the others. Lt. Robert Hill was very badly wounded along with Sergeant Wilson. Sixteen Rangers were hit, but all except Lizotte, who was really down for the count, bravely manned their weapons and hammered the enemy with heavy and sustained fire.

The heavy incoming fire had knocked out every Ranger radio. One PRC-25 had a light glowing in the Frequency Indicator box. Stone, hoping that even though it was damaged it could still transmit, called for help.

Meanwhile back at the Dong Tan Ranger TOC, Huey pilot Warrant Officer LaPotta heard the "May Day" call. He raced to his chopper and took off not even waiting the required five minute engine warm up time in his rush to fly to his besieged Ranger buddies. Stone turned his strobe light on when the circling bird was close. LaPotta turned on his landing lights and came in hot on the small clearing. About 20 feet off the ground the bird clipped a tree with its tail rotor and went into a wild spin, crashing onto its side. The main rotor went flying and the turbine raced out of control as the crew un-assed the chopped yelling, "It's going to blow," "It's going to blow," to Stone and Dennis McNally, who'd raced over to the downed bird to help. When things settled down and LaPotta figured that it wasn't going to explode, he returned to the aircraft and shut it down. The crew then removed the ship's weapons and ammo and joined Stone's people on the perimeter.

Ranger Warren Lizotte died a few hours after he was evacuated back to Dong Tam. Lt Hill, Sergeant Wilson, Ranger Richard Shimel and a few others badly wounded Rangers never returned to the company.

Huey pilot LaPotta was almost court martialed for his heroic, but unauthorized and some say reckless flight. Ranger CO Captain Dale Dickey went to "General Ewell and got the charges thrown out. Ewell well understood Dickey's defense: "Screw the regulations, he was trying to save my men." Stone and Chesser were awarded the Silver Star for their incredible gallantry.

On 10 April 1969, a Hunter Killer team was put together and inserted into a large open rice paddy. SFC Jessie Stephens was the new Operations NCO for Tan An and wanted to see first-hand how the guys operated in the open areas of the Mekong Delta. Other members of the team were Ray Bazini, Chip Crabb, Bill Christiansen, Hilan Jones, and Lonnie Evens. The insertion was uneventful but shortly after all hell broke loose. The patrol had only moved a few meters when a loud explosion was heard. The LRRPs returned automatic weapons into the nearest tree line hoping to hit whoever might be in the area.

Lonnie Evans was killed instantly as a claymore pellet entered his back between the shoulder blades and pierced his heart. Jones was hit in the right buttocks as a pellet went through his thigh and lodge in his scrotum. Two others received small shrapnel wounds.

The evacuation was accomplished in short order and the patrol returned to Tan An. Jones was evacuated to Saigon and then on to Zama Japan.

Ranger missions were diverse and not always done according to the book, one such mission was a rescue. The call for help came to the Rangers and Sergeant Boudreau quickly assembled a team to assist. A vehicle had been ambushed about half way between My Tho and Dong tam and the two occupants were wounded. They were rescued by the Ranger team just minutes after the call was made.

Team 22 had a busy and successful week. On 31 May they destroyed a mortar squad and on June 2, they teamed with gunships to kill 19 VC, just a typical day in the life of a 9th Division Ranger.

Another successful "Parakeet" mission. 21 June was a sad day for Echo Company 75th Rangers. During the conduct of a "parakeet mission, Staff Sergeant Herbert "Frosty" Frost was killed doing what he loved to do; killing the enemy any way he could. A suspected VC was spotted and like they had done so many times before the chopper swooped in and the Rangers were off and running, chasing the VC along a rice paddy dike. The fleeing enemy fired a shot over his shoulder as he was fleeing and got lucky. "Frosty" died doing what he did best.

Company "E" executed the coup of the war when Ranger Mike Kentes zapped the highest racking VC killed during the war, Lt General Hai Tram. On 24 August 1969, during the Toan Thang Offensive in Long An Province. Helicopter gunships from an air cavalry element of the U.S. Army 12th Combat Aviation Group sighted an unknown number of enemy soldiers 11 miles SW of Tra Cu. The gunships engaged the enemy with aerial machinegun and rocket fire.

A short while later a six man Ranger team-- SGTs Jessie Stephens, Christie Valenti, Tom Dineen, Ray Bazini, a former VC named Kiet who was a PRU (Provincal Recon Unit, part of the CIA Project Phoenix Program that was --according to Ranger Cheek-carried out in part by "E" Company) and CPL Mike Kentes, air-assaulted into the vicinity and soon discovered several NVA bodies that had been killed by the Helicopter gunships, and one survivor which Valenti took prisoner. Continuing the sweep they discovered more bodies and one wounded soldier that was trying to unfasten a grenade from his belt. Kentes shot and killed him with two burst from his CAR-15. While searching the body he discovered a 9-MM Czechs made Makarov pistol, the type only carried by senior officers and officials. This is believed to be the only such type of weapon captured in the entire war. A total of nine enemy soldiers were killed and nine weapons captured, along with twenty five pounds of documents.

After the raid the detainee identified himself as a North Vietnamese Army captain and battalion commander. One of the enemy soldiers killed by the Rangers was identified by the captain as Lieutenant General Hai Tram, Commander of the enemy's Sub-Region 3 with several battalions operating in the area of Long An Province. The team was immediately reinserted to find out. Documents found on the body and photographs corroborated the identification of the dead Lt. General. The NVA captain stated that he and the General were on their way to Cambodia for R&R when intercepted by the gunships and Rangers. There were no U.S. casualties in the engagement. General Abrams and the American Ambassador flew in to congratulate the Rangers. This was a big deal. Our getting Tram was like Grant getting Lee or the VC zapping Abrams. Ranger Cheeks recalls, waking up to the sound of someone running through the Ranger barracks back at Tan An saying "Kentes killed a General," I remember mumbling groggily to myself "was it one of ours or one of theirs?"

Team 22, Ralph Funk's old team now led by Stu Koontz, was on Initial Reaction Force Status at Tan An. Mid-afternoon sometime in the fall of 69' a call came in to the TOC about an enemy sighting in a free fire zone in the Plain of Reeds by someone in a chopper. The team was scrambled and was at the chopper pad within seconds and lifted off in pursuit of the elusive foe.

They were vectored into the area by the "higher-higher" who initially made the sighting and off loaded near some heavy Nipa palm. The "Oscar 5 or 6" (either a LTC. Or full bird) came up on the team freg and directed them to a path that led into some very heavy, thick brush and within two meters made a hard right turn.

Koontz though "uh oh," this doesn't look good; I sure could use Nhan (team 22's PRU-a North Vietnam native and Catholic whose parents were killed by the Communists prior to 1954). He saw hand painted "Tu Dia" on a piece of metal somewhat hidden by the foliage, and remembered from his in country indoctrination that it was the Vietnamese word for booby trap. Koontz was convinced he didn't want to go in that Nipa palm without a really good reason and the dude in the chopper hovering at 2000 feet just didn't provide a good enough of one.

Next thing he heard was some squawking on the horn about what's going on down there and what's the hold up? He told the Oscar that they weren't going in there without some good prep fire by Spooky or Cobra and some arty and even a couple of 500 pound napalm drops. That sure as hell didn't go over too well with the colonel and he let Koontz know it. Said he had to go into the Nipa and check it out. He backed off when Koontz suggested he un-ass that chopper and go into the Nipa himself and they would provide covering fire.

Team 22 was on a daytime patrol in a Huey flying alone a waterway with gunships for cover. Don Andrews was in the process of taking over as team leader and Koontz was along to help with the transition. They were going along a blue, when several NVA in a sampan were spotted. The Huey pilot did a quick pull-up and turned to set them down, but when the rotors started chopping tree branches and leaves, the team went ahead and jumped out.

Andrews had on a PRC 77 radio that was previously used by Paul Fitzsimons. The straps were adjusted for him and were caked with dried mud. When Andrews put it on he couldn't adjust it, so the radio hung down low on his waist. When they jumped out, he landed in the mud and sunk knee deep. The radio slammed into the back of his head opening a good size gash in his neck, making a nice cut. We rounded up the NVA and had them choppered off to MI, (Military Intelligence) so they could interrogate them and let em go, or whatever they do (that was always the scuttlebutt!).

Returning to Tan An, the team was walking from the chopper pad through the artillery area, to the main street of the Brigade base camp. As they got to the street, right across from the PX, they saw two things simultaneously. One was the 3rd Brigade/9th Division Commander, the other was two FNG's (f---ing new guy's), with their still green (bright green) fatigues. The FNG's started saluting for all they were worth. The Colonel hollered a greeting to the LRRPs and they hollered back.

The FNG's looked at them: Muddy, bloody (the blood had dried on the side if Andrew's neck and collar), half worn-off camouflage, and probably no complete uniform among them. As he recalls, they were prone to wearing cut-offs and going barefooted.

While many of the directives received were deemed stupid, it was truly believe that many were issued simply because many of the officers making the decisions didn't know how to tactically employ the LRRPs. Colonel Hackworth was right on when he said we were fighting the war using WW 11 tactics. Remember, the LRRP units were on the cutting edge of new war fighting tactics.

Many of the things they did had never been done before. Then throw in the factor of ticket punches and awards, there were tremendous pressures brought to bear. Had it not been for "Top" Press keeping the LRRP officers straight, they may have gotten into many conflicts as well.

Norm Breece had taken over team 11 after graduating from Recondo School, when Curtis Daniels was killed. One of the first missions for his team was a stay behind with a line unit from the 3rd Brigade. During the visual recon Norm gleaned right away that it was going to be extremely difficult to find a good "hide" in this highly populated area. The mission was to collect some high ranking VC/ NVA that was meeting in the small village northwest of Tan Tru. He dropped off the tail gunner into the hide position at last light. Immediately there were children in the areal looking for the team. *A couple of young girls* walked into the position and had to be kept with the team until they were ready to move on the hooch.

It wasn't very long when night calm was saturated with the heavy noise of mechanized tracks. Norm called to Weids & Stinky who were monitoring the radio at base camp and asked them to identify the mechanized unit to the South. They called back saying there were no friendlies in the area. That was confusing to Breece as he was somewhat confident that NVA armor hadn't traveled that far south. They continued to hear the tracks coming closer and closer, but higher continued to deny their existence. At 2000 hours the team moved into the village, taking along the kids they had acquired. The hooch was a negative, but the most elaborate one he had seen during his tour to date. The cat had some serious cash. The tracks could be heard moving into their final night position, gunning the Detroit's as they came on line.

Releasing the girls, the team began moving west from the village and into the night position. Kentes was walking point as they broke from the midst of the last hooch, when a round snapped by his face. He hit the deck and everyone though he was joking around. Breece told him to get up and move out, when he immediately received another round right by his snoot. Again, for some reason, Breece hadn't heard the round and summarily chewed on Kentes and told him to get moving. They had only moved far enough for the entire team to get alongside a big dike line running east and west when all hell broke loose.

The tracks unloosed a major barrage from their 50s. The ground actually felt as if an earthquake was occurring. The ground was being ground away and flying everywhere. Kentes and Valenti had "unders," Cheek had his M-79, Root, and Phouc M-16s and Breece carried his Car-15. Everyone with the 40s were told to put as many rounds in the air as possible, they managed 3 in the short seconds before the first round hit the tree line about 400-500 yards to the south. They all fired one magazine of 5.56 to break contact, got up and ran as hard as they could to the west. It worked, as the tracks lit up the area just to their rear. With contact broken, they continued to low crawl along the dike.

Breece had been on the radio with the Fire Support Base trying to get the goofy ARVNs off their backsides, when a marking round went off. Willie Peet, 200 feet up. The big gun were firing from Tu Tua. Norm had previously fired with the Red Legs over there and quickly went up on their push telling them to check fire as it was friendlies they would be firing up. They acknowledged and initiated the check fire.

Higher told him that they wanted him to move the team to a position to the west. He came back much too aggressively and said a few expletives that later got his butt in a sling, but they finally sent a chopper out and extracted them. The run to the chopper seemed like an eternity, knowing the trigger happy ARVNs were just a few hundred yards to the south. Needless to say, he had some choice words for them back at the ranch.

Around that same time, they pulled a security mission with three arty guys, a major and two enlisted guys with the biggest starlight scope Breece had ever seen. They were to set up at the junction of a major dike line. Breece had a good visual recon and planned how they would conduct the mission. The problems began when they hit the LZ, close to last light. Immediately the major had the misconception that he was in charge. He wanted to split the teams and move several hundred yards apart to wait for dark. Breece immediately nixed that idea and told the major in no uncertain terms that if he wanted to split up, he could move his people to an area of cover to their northwest and he would set up security there in a defendable position. The major was ticked off and moved into his position.

It started to rain and for a while it was miserable. Breece had carefully watched where the major had gone and when it became dark he moved out. They circled his position to the south and came in from the west. By now, the moon was giving some good light and they showed the red legs why they were good at what they did. Sneaking up behind the major and tapped him on the shoulder thinking he would probably wet his pants. They moved out to the preplanned junction of the dikes, set them up to watch, and all went to sleep. Man that was a big starlight scope!

We pulled another stay behind with a unit from 3rd Bde. This one was really fun. We took trucks out to the jump off point and once again were the tail gunners of the file. We were moving thru a large Village, I don't recall which; all of us were at high alert as a whole company had walked through there already. We were walking parallel to a large canal when a gook stood up right in the bushes beside the hardball. I heard 6 M16 safeties, click, click, click, etc. We didn't fire the dude up because we recognized the Chu Hoi from the line unit. That dump almost cost him his life. The interesting thing was the grunts right in front of us seemed oblivious to him.

We continued into the night, marching toward the NW. We had been traveling about an hour and a half when I heard something from the west. I halted the grunts near me and the team and we laid down. Whatever it was coming, they sounded like a herd of elephants. I called the CO and told him of the movement, and he halted his formation. The noise stopped. Here we are out in the middle of nowhere with a point element of this company lost. I told the CO the noise had quit, that his point element was walking right into his flank element and to pass the word not to fire us up. He claimed he knew where he was at and it couldn't be him. One of the platoon leaders had been listening to our discussion and moved back to my position. We discussed the situation; he called the CO and confirmed the snafu. The CO's solution was to have all of the men in the formation continue to follow the man in front of him and come back to the spot we were at. I told him my team would remain and wait for them to wade through two blue lines and link back up. We had a very pointed discussion, but I remained there.

After quite a while, the tail element was back to our position, and we continued north. After another half hour or so the CO me called up to his position. He was under his poncho with a red lens flashlight. We discussed our position and he was lost. I tried to tactfully show him where we were but my patience was really thin. Finally, I went up on Arty's push and called for two marking rounds on adjacent grids, did a resection, and found out I was about 150 meters from where I thought I was. Man was that young Cpt mad. We dropped off at our mission site shortly thereafter. It turned out to be a dumping point on a major dike line close to a village. The rats were as big as house cats. Man to this day I still can't stand rats. They were crawling across our legs and feet. They weren't scared of anything. They would jump when you poked them with the barrel of the 16 but would come right back.

This mission really took on another twist. We were to move to an LZ for pick up at first light. So, we move into position and waited for the sun. About 0600, I got a call informing me a 25th ID unit was in big contact and no air assets were available until later. Well we were out of water, and had no rations because this was to be an overnighter. Shame on us. We waited until around 1000 hrs. Still no choppers. We were about 700 meters from the blue line that run right by the unit we went out with. We moved to the river and after a couple of shots across the bow, Papa-san pulled his sampan over to the bank and gave us a ride to the village close to the TOC. As I recalled we paid the old boy a few MPC and he was giggly.

The Major we ran into when we walked into the TOC to borrow his land line to arrange transportation back to Tan An wasn't very amused. This was the same bugger eater that couldn't get us a ride home, but was really upset we found our own way. He summarily chewed my backside. Well that day he discovered the truth of the axiom, "Where there is a LRRP there is a way."

"1970"

COMPILED BY

BRENT GULICK

Many thoughts raced through Lieutenant Walker's mind as he waited in the Naval Operations Center at Ben Luc, Vietnam. The young Engineer Officer was contemplating the mission with which he was soon to be involved. He was waiting to meet Lieutenant Toschik, Operations Officer, Company E (Ranger) 75th Infantry. The Rangers had a special interest in Walker; his company could furnish them with small, fast boats (Kenner Ski Barges) which they needed for their operation AQUABUSH. Although he had never participated in the operation, Walker had heard many stories about the missions. Tonight he was going to accompany the Rangers, on an "Aqua bush" to get a feel of the mission and to determined how his boats and crews would fit into future operations.

Toschik soon arrived and wasted no time in introducing Walker to the aqua bush concepts. He began the briefing on the way to the Warf: "We've been giving Charlie hell along his sampan highways and in his Nipa Palm sanctuaries. The Regional and Popular Forces and our ground pounders haven't let the enemy out of the Nipa lately. The "old man" got with the Navy and worked out a combined operation- the Aqua bush-whereby we can go after the VC in their own back yard."

As the two officers reached the water round, Toschik pointed to a cluster of small outboard motor boats, similar to those used for fishing and water skiing back in the States. "It took too much work to get our boats rigged like we want them, and to get our techniques worked out with the Navy. All of our men are swimmers and each is cross-trained as a pilot, in fact each is cross trained in many skills. These boats are the Navy's Boston Whalers with fiberglass hulls and twin 40 HP engines which can attain a speed of 30 knots and get on a plane in 10 meters. One boat has its own electric starter a necessity in our operation. We tried a big 85 HP engine but it didn't have the power of two 40s, nor did it have a reserve propulsion capability. We designed that M-60 mount to give a low silhouette for the machine gunner and to keep the center of gravity down. The pilot's PRC-77 is strapped to the steering console. Thus far, a shortage of repair parts has been our greatest problem. We resorted to cannibalization in an effort to keep two boats operational at all times. Now, the Navy is pulling out of this immediate area. That's why we need your help, they are going to take their boats with them."

Walker thought about his Kemmer Ski Barges and compared them with the Whalers. The Ski Barge has a metal hull and is a little larger craft; the capabilities are about the same. His boats also use twin 40s and each boat had an electric starter. The Ski Barges' machinegun mounts were taller than the Navy ones-they'd have to be shortened. He explained to Toschik that the boats would interchange, and that there should be no difficulty making the switch. The Engineers had an outboard motor mechanic, by MOS, and a Prescribed Load List. Maintained should be no problem. He was intrigued by the mission, however, and quizzed Toschik for more information.

"The whalers are always used in pairs for mutual support. The Navy provides two crewmen- a pilot and a machine gunner. We split a six-man Ranger team between two boats, and we're ready for action. Each Ranger wears camouflaged fatigues, a black shirt, a black hat or head band, and some captured equipment to confuse Charlie, who is rather easily fooled in his watery haven. Virtually all our boat ambushes are sprung at extremely close range. One night while we were listening and waiting to move inland, a VC walked up to the boat and squatted down into the muzzle of a shotgun. We keep plenty of grenades handy on our load bearing equipment and in the boat; all guys have 50 round magazines filled with tracers for the initial impact- we don't stick around very long after the first magazine."

Toschik explained that even though the Rangers carried a shotgun and M79 in each boat, they seldom used the grenade launchers. "The Nipa is nearly always too close and thick. We carry Claymore Mines rigged on long stakes but, in many cases, contact is made before we have a chance to put them out."

The Rangers checked load bearing equipment, weapons, claymore mines, radios and boats before departing on Aqua bush missions. "When departing for a mission, we usually follow in the wake of patrol boats or whatever crafts the Navy has going our way. Actually, we don't really need the noise screen because these engines can cut back to a troll speed with less noise than a motorized sampan. Charlie listens for the big boats and makes his crossings as they pass around a bend; we have a few early evening contacts, on our way to a night location, by following about 500 meters behind big boats." Toschik related.

He explained that the Navy had long known many of Charlie's favorite crossing sites and often received good targets from agent reports of enemy activity along the river. Third Brigade, 9th Infantry Division had patterned NVA infiltration routes which included water path is well as numerous fords and shuttle points. Also, when airmobile units witnessed Charlie's disappearing act during the day sweep, the small Navy/Ranger task force reacted by slipping back into the area after dark and after Charlie crawled from his crawfish hole.

Walker listened intently as the Ranger Lieutenant explained the actual ambush technique: "The ATL (Assistant Team Leader) sets up his boat in a supporting position where the stream or canal junctions with the river. The TL (Team Leader) has his pilot slowly back his Whaler up the tributary, never more than 50 meters. That flat bottom boat sounds just like a sampan as the water laps at its hull in the darkness. Once in position, and after a short listening period, the Rangers wade inland about 30 meters and set up. As movement is detected, the old heart rate accelerates. You would be surprised how freely and boldly the enemy moves in the mud and Nipa after dark with flash lights, whistles, talking and shouting.

The team leader initiates the ambush when he sees figures moving toward his position, many times talking or signaling to him. The center Ranger tosses grenades and saves his weapon to cover the hasty movement back to the boat, where the machine gunner is firing in support. Once the Rangers make contact they retreat back to the boat while drawing the enemy to chase them. As they tumble back to the boat, which starts at the sound of the first shot, the machine gunner on the boat opens up on the target. He then signals for the support boat to open fire on the tracer impact area.

The pilot keeps the boat in position against the tide and current by holding onto Nipa branches until his machine gunner opens fire. Than it takes a skilled pilot to steer and throttle a low draft boat into a pick up position. With all aboard, little time is lost in making a speedy get away to open water. "Walker thought about the Aqua bush and mentally evaluated his personnel and their ability to perform this type of mission. His people were good and they had experience, but he would have to devote initial training time to refining extraction techniques.

Toschik broke his thought: "You will have to evaluate tide data. We learned that lesson the hard way; getting stuck in Charlie country can be a nerve raking experience. Also, you'll want to be aware of moon position to take advantage of bank shadows."

The team leader can call for gunship, artillery, or gunboat support with his PRC-77. We will have your support boat radio monitor headquarters' frequency at all times. Prior to each mission, the team leader coordinates directly with artillery, navel gunships, naval gunboats, and with any units, such as SEALs or Riverine Forces, operating on the river the night of his operation.

To avoid setting a pattern, we make full use of the hundreds of miles of connecting waterways accessible to us, and we make all reconnaissance by air, never by boat. We never ambush the same location! We use Ranger teams which alternate their nights between ambushing and drying out from the previous sleepless night spent in mud and water.

"Occasionally, we react to a Navy contact as an assault element or blocking force. Also, we have had some luck reacting to radar sightings of sampans crossing the river. We like to leave a sniper on the ATL's boat to scan the opposite bank for easy targets on foot or in sampan. A little light reflection off the water considerably increases a starlight scope capability. The sniper can fire at will, as sound direction is not well detected over water."

"The best way to break you into our operation is to show you. I will take Team 17 out tonight and give Sergeant Bryan a rest. He has a knack for this type of operations and has been very successful with it. It takes a team leader with steady nerves to execute the ambush in a timely way and not be caught in a compromising situation. As you will see, this is a risky mission; however, surprise and firepower are our equalizers. You will have to be my machine gunner. The Whaler will carry only five men and retain minimum safe power. Don't worry, we'll check you out, and Chief Slater, who helped pioneer our techniques will give you assistance if you need it."

After chow, Walker joined the little task force as it checked weapons, motors, radios and equipment. With everything ready, it headed north in the vanishing wake of an Assault Support Patrol boat escorting two Tango boats of Vietnamese Marines. Lieutenant Walker tried to visualize the target, previously briefed as one of several canals in an area of numerous, recent DUFFLEBAG activations, Brigade Operations radio reported that the radar sight at Thu Thua Canal junction reported a sampan crossing into the Eagles Beak from the Plain of Reeds, right on target. Two small craft quickly pulled alongside the Tangos and the pilots prepared to slip into the bank shadows.

The target canal identified and the support boat positioned, Toschik's Whaler sleekly glided under the low hanging Nipa branches. The three Rangers gingerly slid into the water and moved into the pitch stillness of the Nipa grove. Soon, only the slapping of the walking fish could be detected around the Ranger position. Dim lights appeared and slowly moved toward the blacken bushwhackers. The radio suddenly came to life.

"17, this is Swordfish, over."

"Fish, this is 17, over"

"This is Fish, I have a sampan, about thirty meters out, moving in my direction."

Toward 17 ALPHA's position

"This is 17, hold off, I have three lights converging on my position. Stand-by to blow and make it wait."

"17 ALPHA, 17, are you monitoring, over?"

"17 ALPHA, Rodger, over."

Suddenly the bank void of the night became a psychotic happening as the three Rangers opened fire and took the opportunity to hurriedly splash back to their impatiently waiting cohorts. After clearing the canal, Lieutenant Toschik directed fire and adjusted illumination and H.E. while awaiting the Navy gunships which were previously alerted by his ATL.

He remarked to his new friend, "Well Lieutenant Walker, you did a good job shooting up that sampan. Now that you have had a firsthand look, what do you think of our Aqua bush?

"A little hairy but it is hard to complain about success," was his reply.

The following incident happened sometime in 1970 east of Tan An Vietnam. It involved one ambush team from Echo company 75th Infantry (Airborne Rangers) of the 3rd Brigade 9th Infantry Division and a couple of small navy boats from the Mobile Riverine Force assigned to Tan An along with their navy drivers. To best recollection each vessel was about 18 feet long, had twin outboard engines and a machine turret in the middle of each boat.

We boarded the boats in Tan An and headed down river east of Tan An for several miles in broad daylight. After an uneventful ride of several miles the navy dropped us off on the river bank next to a hooch that had a clear beach where we could climb off without difficult. I say this as opposed to being dropped off of PBRs in the Nipa bushes and mud which was a different exercise and it could take one or two guys just to assist another person back onto a boat.

After disembarking the navy boats left us and returned to Tan An. Chuck Watson our Team leader immediately called in a marker round to verify our location. Also with us on this night was Lt. Gulick, our platoon lieutenant. We waited on the river bank until dark then moved out across a dry rice paddy eventually getting to our ambush location where we set up in typical fashion. As it turned out it was an uneventful evening and in the morning we moved back to the same location where the navy boats had dropped us off.

We ended up spending most of the day on the river bank waiting for the navy boats to return. I have no idea why it took them all day to return but the day ended up to be one of pleasure for us. We spent the day relaxing on the river bank and taking photos of each other. We also kept cool by swimming in the river most of the day just waiting for our ride to return. Eventually at dusk the boats showed up and off we headed back to Tan An. It got pitch dark right away and navigation became difficult. The first boat turned on a strobe light for the second boat to follow. To this day the wisdom of the first boat displaying a strobe light for the second boat to follow has bothered me; for at the time I remember thinking how fortunate I was to be in the second boat. I was also wondering how the driver of the first boat could tell where to go and then realized he was following the silhouette of the tree line on both sides of the river. Between the trees on either side of the river was a beautiful sky full of bright stars or it was this path of stars we were following back to base.

Suddenly the strobe light went out. Immediately the navy driver slowed our boat down and with the decrease in rpms the engine noise became lower and we could hear the guys in the first boat yelling excitedly but we couldn't see anything. Suddenly we hit a rice paddy dike head on just as the boat ahead of us had but at a much reduced speed. The first boat had hit the dike at full speed and went over the dike stopping flat against a second dike. The boat was literally wedged in between two dikes. Fortunately no one had been hurt, but they were sure shook up. *As* it turned out there was no tree line to follow when they hit the dike because the rice paddy came right down to the river's edge and the two dikes separated the river from the paddy. *As* a result the driver drove into it head on.

So there we were, everyone standing around assessing the situation. I was standing on the second dike to see one side of the boat which was wedged in. Another guy, a new kid we had on our team who was a f--k up and became nicknamed Daffy Duck was standing immediately in front of the wedged boat on the same dike as I was. When I looked over towards Daffy I saw him throw something at me. It turned out to be a live smoke grenade which hit me on my leg and bounced on the ground resting on my feet. This stupid act of his immediately pissed me off, so I picked it up and threw it back at him with the intention of it burning him good. The grenade hit him in the neck, bouncing off and into the wedged boat. Of course the wedged boat was full of nothing but spilled gasoline and tons of ammunition scattered about including but not limited to light antitank weapons, hand grenades, M60 machine gun belts, phosphorous grenade, claymore mines, etc. Remember we were still shaking off the cobwebs of the accident when this occurred. Well gasoline, ammunition and hot smoke grenades don't mix and so the fireworks began.

All of us immediately ran for cover behind the dikes and watched the fireworks for some time. It was quite a show, lasting a long time and of course it goes without saying that the boat was not just a total loss but there was nothing left of it by the time it was over. I thought I was going to L. B. J. for the incident but nothing ever came of it. I wasn't even questioned for that matter. It was just another day at the office. Eventually we got a ride out by chopper back to Tan An for a warm meal and shower.

On 30 April, while serving as Team Leader on an overnight ambush operation assisted by U.S. Navy Patrol Boats, Sergeant Bob Bryan positioned a three man element of the team about 75 meters from the shore, leaving the remaining members in the boat. Spotting approximately five enemy soldiers 200 meters from his location, Sgt Bryan immediately exposed himself to initiate contact with the enemy, eliminating one instantly. While leading his men through the intense hostile fire he heard someone whistle. Again spotting another enemy soldier twenty meters from his position, he exposed himself to hurl a grenade at the insurgent, eliminating him. He then directed his team back to the boat. Upon reaching the craft, two enemy sampans were observed on the river coming toward them. *As* the insurgents initiated contact, Sergeant Bryan once again exposed himself to the enemy fusillade to direct the fire of his team.

The four enemy personnel aboard the sampans were eliminated. Later, while sweeping the contact area, the team again received intense fire from an enemy soldier concealed in the Nipa palm, within ten meters of the Ranger team. Reacting instantly to the critical danger, Sergeant Bryan charged forward and eliminated the insurgent at point blank range with rifle fire. The team was extracted without further incident.

11 June 1970 while his team was proceeding along a river bank, Sergeant Bryan observed an enemy soldier to his front. The enemy attempted to react, but Sergeant Bryan immediately eliminated him. As the team moved further along, Sgt Bryan observed two more enemy soldiers on the opposite shore. Without regard for his personal safety, he immediately moved to an exposed position and eliminated one while another team member fatally wounded the other. Shortly thereafter, the team encountered three more enemy soldiers about fifteen meters to their front. Sgt Bryan and other team members immediately rushed the enemy, eliminating them before they could fire back when a booby trap denoted causing several members of the team to receive fragmentation wounds. Sergeant Bryan without hesitation applied first aid, then, directed a helicopter to pick up the wounded. Sergeants Bryan's actions were in keeping with the highest traditions of the military service and reflect great credit upon himself, his unit and the United States Army. Sergeant Bryan continued to lead his Ranger Team 17 in the warrior tradition, leading by example, and inspiring his fellow rangers to give 100% and then some.

On13 July 1970, just 24 days away from Robert's departure from Vietnam, he was killed in action by enemy ground fire, while conducting a visual reconnaissance from a light observation helicopter preparing for yet another mission.

On 11 August 1970 1st Lieutenant Mark Toschik was killed in action in Dinh Province in the Republic of South Vietnam and was posthumously awarded the Silver Star Medal for gallantry in action as well as the National Order of Vietnam, Fifth Class. The circumstances of the action leading to these awards are as follows: Lt Toschik had made an aerial reconnaissance by helicopter early in the day to determine night ambush positions. He was inserting one of his teams just before dark and was flying in the insertion helicopter, while his platoon sergeant flew in another cover helicopter.

Lt. Toschik had inserted his team which had moved out quickly to avoid detection. As the helicopter lifted off, it came under point blank fire from the rear. The action was quick and fierce. LT Toschik was the only one on the ground or in either helicopter who saw the enemy. He must have seen the muzzle flashes and immediately returned fire. No one knows when he was hit, but because the contact was brief and the rescue swift, he must have been hit with the initial burst. LT Toschik fought back savagely with all his resources. He expended his 30 round magazine, and 20 round magazines of two additional M-16 rifles in the helicopter. He fired all the rounds of his 9mm pistol and to attest to the relative closeness of the encounter, he threw the empty pistol at them. He then ripped the .38 caliber pistol from the co-pilots shoulder holster and emptied it before the helicopter hit the ground. It is difficult to imagine how quickly this all took place. LT Toschik helicopter had hardly touched down and lifted off when it was brought down, having traveled less than the length of a football field, in a crescent arc. The support helicopter flying in the same arc pattern landed swiftly alongside the downed craft. Upon impact, LT Toschik, who was not wearing a seatbelt, dismounted and unstrapped the two wounded pilots and pulled them to safety. He then moved around the far side of the downed helicopter searching for other crew members. He could go no farther and collapsed on the spot where his platoon sergeant found his body.

As the war in Vietnam was coming to an end by order of President Nixon, E Company Rangers began stand down procedures and was formerly deactivated in November, 1970. The 9th Division LRRP/Rangers left a legacy of courage and sacrifice having lost 27 men in combat, and 1 man from the effects of the war. No other combat recon units waged reconnaissance and intelligence-gathering operations under circumstances more difficult than those of the 9th Infantry Division in Vietnam. Torrential rains and year round water exposed the LRRP/Rangers to high rates of disabling skin disease. They often suffered extensive inflammatory lesions and rampant skin infections. Despite this, the LRRP/Rangers were on the cutting edge of new war fighting tactics and conducted some of the hairiest missions of the war. They also had a great psychological impact on the enemy often attacking him in his own "backyard." They created sound tactical doctrine and imaginative techniques in adjusting to the Mekong Delta and applied undeviating pressure against the Viet Cong havens and their supply lines through the unit's term of duty in Vietnam. The Rangers were hated, feared and respected so much by the enemy that bounties were offered from $1,000 to $2,500, at a time when a citizen was working for about 85 cents a day. This was the same bounty offered for a captured or killed American Colonel.

RECOLLECTIONS OF A LRRP FIRST SERGEANT

BY

ROY D NELSON

It has been almost 30 years since I first arrived in Vietnam in 1966 as the Operations NCO of the 9th Division Cavalry Squadron. I have since come to realize that memories fade and history of units are diminished forever by the failure to record the stories of first hand experiences. It is for this reason that I have written the following. May it encourage others to do so.

I joined the 9th Infantry Division Long Range Patrol (LRP) at Camp Bear Cat in March 1967. I had recently had a personal conflict with my Squadron Commander and was summarily reassigned to the LRP as a First Sergeant. The unit had been attached to the Delta Troop of the Squadron during its building and training phase. It was less than a platoon in strength and lacked the weapons, radio, compasses and other equipment necessary to carry out patrols. Since there was no TOE (Table of Organizational Equipment) for the unit, it was difficult to acquire the basic equipment, but somehow we prevailed.

In the interim we trained, got physically fit, ran missions and searched for volunteers while we tried to develop confidence and veracity with the divisional operations staff. The process involved weeding out the unqualified and determining who had what it took to lead the patrols.

Recollections of a LRRP First Sergeant

My intention as First Sergeant was to teach the same fundamentals taught by the MACV Recondo School at Nha Trang, and to instill the basic instinct of survival into each and every LRRP who volunteered for the company. I've always subscribed to General George Patton's philosophy, "You don't fight to die for your country, you fight to make the other SOB die for his country." For some reason it made sense to me. I strongly believed that you could do this job without getting decisively engaged with the enemy.

We formed five-man recon teams, and sometimes went out with only four men in the Mekong Delta. By July 1967, we had formalized as the 9th Infantry Division Long Range Patrol (LRPD) and were assigned to Division Headquarters & Headquarters Company. We had grown to over 100 enlisted men and five officers. We had even constructed our own compound with semi-permanent wooden barracks along the wire near the Replacement Company at Bear Cat.

As we became more proficient at what we did, I began to realize that the LRRPs were not necessarily the best persons or the finest soldiers. They were men who were just the best at what they did. They had to have patience and a good instinct for survival in the type of covert warfare we were involved in. They also had to have the ability to accept danger and hardship without succumbing to the stress that went along with it. That were good at what they did and they liked it. Some of our best LRRPs extended their tours, and not all of them made it home.

My recollections include working with the Australian Special Air Service (SAS) in Phouc Tuy Province. Sergeant Ray Hulin was leading a team in contact with a VC unit, and was trying to break contact to get to their extraction site. I was with the CP at Nui Dat with the 1st Australian Task Force when we got word to provide a reaction force for the team. The Hueys were ready to go when we arrived at the pad. I personally selected the LRRPs I wanted to go. When I turned around I saw two new men, Hilan Jones and John Dunlap, who had just arrived in the unit that morning. They were aboard the Hueys, and trying to avoid my gaze. I knew then I had made a good choice during the selection process---they had the "right stuff" to be LRRPs.

The Australian SAS were hard drinking, hard fighting soldiers. Their methods of long range patrolling were different from ours. When they made contact with the enemy, they attacked with everything they had. They carried those heavy 7.62mm FN-SLRs (Self Loading Rifle). Their rationale was to make the enemy break contact by disrupting his ability to go on the offensive. If they ran low on ammo and grenades, they threw rocks or anything else that was handy. A lot of the SAS were veterans of fighting communist insurgencies in Malaya and other hot spots.

The U.S. Navy SEALs were another wild bunch. They operated in the Rung Sat Special Zone and were something else when it came to taking the war to the enemy. The Rung Sat was a series of salt water swamps choked with mangroves. The SEAL teams did not maintain radio contact while on patrol. They were a little crazy- maybe even demented- but they got the job done. They remained with the same team during their six-month tours of duty, and I believed this was a real boom to team integrity. They were highly skilled and well trained, and had the best equipment. I really like the Stoner Weapons System the SEALs used. It was deadly in close combat. We picked up a lot of our camouflage jungle fatigues from the SEALs, uniforms we couldn't get from the Army. I didn't envy their AO (Area of Operations) though- too much water. They were normally inserted and extracted by water/ utilizing a number of river patrol craft such as the PBR, which were low draft boats, water jet driven and very fast.

I remember returning once from a mission board a Huey helicopter. My team had spent a day and a half avoiding VC units actively looking for us. We had managed to avoid firing even a single round, although enemy soldiers had been firing warning and signal shots throughout our AO. We spent the last night listening to VC movements all around us as they searched for us with flashlights. After all the anxiety and stress from being too long in close proximity to danger and death, the tension was broken on the return trip to Bear Cat when Noonan leaned forward and took the tape off the face of my military issue watch and yelled in my ear, "We'll get back in time to watch Combat on the TV." It was just another way of coping with what we endured on those missions.

Part of my job was to observe the individual and team training of the unit and accompany the teams as an observer to critique the methods and results. Gradually we gained a good reputation with Division. But it was difficult to overcome their natural animosity against elite units. We had to develop a "believability quotient" just to sell our results to the people at division G-2.Many times I had to listen to staff officers remarking at a debriefing that there were no VC in an area just patrolled by a LRRP team- it just being nothing but "LRRP Bullshit." Gradually, our results were believed when a follow-up Arc Light strike or a ground unit sweep verified that the enemy was indeed there.

As we got better at what we did, we expanded our horizons. We operated with the US NAVY SEALs IN THE Rung Sat Special Zone; we stirred up the Plain of Reeds; we scouted out the defoliated areas of War Zone D; and even invaded Thoi Son Island (VC Island) to cut the VC's lines of communication.

I led the first LRP teams in to the Plain of Reeds and on to Thoi San Island. These actions probably alerted the local VC of the small unit activity in their areas. Sergeant Ray Hulin led a team on to "VC Island" during a night insertion. They had no sooner dismounted from the landing craft when the VC opened up with machine gun fire and rocket- propelled grenades. The Navy crew ducked for cover and backed the landing craft away from the bank. The LRRPs on board returned fire using the mounted machine-guns and their individual weapons. I remember Staff Sergeant Cottrell burring the barrel up on a .30 caliber light machine gun at the bow position. Fortunately, no one was injured and the team jettisoned gear and swam out to be picked up. This response to enemy fire was instinctive and not ordered by anyone. Another example of these kinds of men.

In spite of all the mundane requirements of soldiering, we still found time to enjoy our free time. Remember, combat is 99% boredom and 1% pure panic. So we took full advantage of the breaks in mission and preparation. We had our cookouts, beer drinking, and resting and ferocious "touch" football games. These games sometimes became more "tackle and get even" events than football contest. I was a young First Sergeant and participated in the games, taking my lumps and bruises without complaint. I can recall no instances of personal dislikes among the members of the unit. At least none were brought to my attention. We had the usual rebel-rousers and guardhouse lawyers in the company. For the most part, we were just too worn down. I had gone from 180 pounds on my arrival in Vietnam to 150 pounds when I rotated out.

This unit eventually became Co E (LRP), 50th Infantry (Abn) on 20th December 1967, and later Co E (Rgr), 75th Infantry (Abn) on 1st February 1970. The unit suffered 26 KIA, including one MIA, during its tour of combat duty.

So much for my misgivings as to the survivability of a LRRP. Apparently, the General Patton philosophy had some effect. There were no KIAs during my tenure as First Sergeant.

I had personally forecast that a company reunion could probably be held in a phone booth rented from AT&T. I was wrong.

I remember the unit NCOs and those who came as privates and grew to NCO rank. Staff Sergeants Richard Cottrell, Arlyn Wieland, Robert Syndram, Elbert Walden and Gregory Nizialek provided the early guidance and training that formed this group of men to a cohesive results-oriented unit. Others were Sergeants Emory Parrish, Johnston Dunlop, Hilan Jones, Bob Hernandez, Ray Hulin, Mike Patrick, Herbert Frost, and Howard Munn, and a host of others since names not remembered, but never forgotten. The officers provided the buffer between us and the higher echelons. They kept the unit reputation intact, and even built on it. Clancy Matsuda, the commanding officer, and I were reunited at a company reunion in 1993. Every time I attend a reunion I come across someone who reinforces my fading memories. I have met some of the wives and children of those young warriors who served themselves and their country so well. I will always be proud of them.

AFTER VIETNAM

BY

ROY BARLEY

When I left RVN on the 1st of October 1968 my thoughts were bittersweet. I had completed my obligation to my country and would soon be a civilian again. I had a fiancée that I was looking forward to seeing again and holding her close. But, I thought of the men I was leaving behind and vowed to stay in touch. I honestly thought I would. I also just wanted to settle down and catch up on two years of my life that seemed lost. I also thought that many returning veterans felt as I did and that they also wanted to forget that past year of hell. I remember wanting to meet some of those hippy bastards that were spitting on uniforms and looked forward to that confrontation at the Port of Authority station in New York. Remembering how much it hurt to see those bastards waving the flag of the Viet Cong in Life Magazine at the 1968 Democratic National Convention in Chicago. I really wanted to extract a price from those assholes. That was not to happen as my folks drove from Cornwall, NY to pick me up at Ft. Dix, NJ over my protest.

As the years passed, thoughts of RVN never faded from my mind. The sheer terror of being ambushed: the stress of being out in Indian Territory with just 4 other men; the life altering effects of combat and the memory of guys who died fighting for each other. I would get very angry around anniversary dates and not really know why. I had stayed in contact with my Platoon Sgt. Greg Nizialek, who lived in Buffalo,

NY. I ended up graduating from College in Buffalo and settling down. It was there a very strange set of circumstances occurred that would send me back to Vietnam in March of 1996.

Greg, who remained in the National Guard, and I would talk on occasion about what he heard from whom and what happened to guys from the unit. One time he and his lovely wife Shirley came over for dinner and he brought a ton of pictures and we discussed the good times and bad. He was particularly concerned about what Ken Lancaster's mother knew and what the Army told her. Ken was a member of our unit who had been attending the MACV Recondo School in Na Trang when he fell from the skid of a helicopter at over 1,000 foot altitude. He was listed as MIA but all of the team members felt that he had been killed instantly.

Our discussion centered on what his Mother knew or did not know. We had this discussion a number of times over the years and I had gotten involved with the formation of a VVA Chapter in Springville, NY. I put it into the back of my mind to try to contact her but it was not my number 1item to do on my list.

In, I believe it was 1986 or maybe 1987; I went to the VVA National Convention in Washington, DC on behalf of our chapter. I also wanted to see the Wall and get some etchings off the wall of men I knew. While there I was able to make contact with one of the officers of the MIA/POW league of families and she told me she would check their data base to see if Mrs. Lancaster was listed. The next day she told me that she was and I was to write a letter to her, place it in a stamped, non-sealed envelope. Then send the unsealed letter to their attention and they would forward it on. A few days after arriving home I did so. In short time I received a phone call from Mrs. Lancaster that went on for hours, I promised her that I would try to find out information on Kenny if I ever went back to RVN. I knew that was a long shot but maybe someday.

As the VVA Chapter President I was amazed at the number of different magazines and newsletters that we received. I made an effort to go thru each one in search of anything that would lead me to former comrades. That need to reconnect was burning up inside me until the day I saw an ad in one of the newsletters that called for former LRRP/ LRP /Rangers to join an organization called the 75th Ranger Regiment INC. I had heard that our LRP Company had become a Ranger unit shortly after I left but never had any proof. The ad had been placed by Al Bartz of Avo, NY in early 1989. I immediately called his phone number and spoke to a guy who was as excited to hear from someone he never knew as I was to find a kindred spirit. He told me about the organization that he placed the ad for, and spoke of their first reunion the year before in Georgia. He let me knew that the 9th Division had some fellows there and had the name of the unit director, Mike Patrick. I immediately sent out as much information about my service in the company along with the application and dues. A few weeks later I got my membership card in the mail. Wow, what a feeling that I may be able to reconnect with old friends thru this organization. Al Brartz died a few months later but I was very thankful that he had placed that ad.

During 1989 and 1990 I tried to find as many members of the unit that I could but success was fair. I wanted to attend the 1990 Reunion in Colorado but I just was not ready for that yet. I did manage to locate Tony Hanlon in PA and had a great meeting with him. My request for a list of members of the unit was knocked down by the President of the Association, Bob Gilbert. I knew that the only way we could start to locate people would be to get copies of orders along with the list maintained by the Association. In early 1992 I received phone calls from Rick Ehrler, Ralph Harter and Bruce Sartwell about the coming reunion at Ft Benning. I had mixed emotions about going to that reunion; what nightmares might surface; did I really want to open that chapter of my life again? After all I had been very successful in life, graduate degree; well respected in my job; head of two separate Veteran's organization; Vice president of the Niagara Frontier Vietnam Veterans Leadership Council; elected to the local school board and elected to the position of Vice President of the Board. Yet it was very difficult to take that first step. After prodding from the three above I made a commitment to go. I had been in contact with Greg Nizalek and he also was going. It was time to take that first step.

Bonding of Warriors

As the date for the reunion grew closer my anxiety grew more intense. My wife encouraged me to make the trip. I kept finding excuses not to go, but when the tickets arrived I knew that I had to go. The night before the trip I could not sleep. Memories of Vietnam were swirling in my head. Thoughts of guys that were killed while I was there came flooding into my mind. I also knew that if they were still alive they would make the trip. It occurred to me that all I had accomplished in life I did with their memory pushing me on. I caught the plane to Atlanta and then a commuter plane to Columbus. On the small commuter plane I sat next to a young lady who was traveling to see her fiancée who was completing Ranger School, When our small plane caught the wake of a much larger plane and dropped a few hundred feet like a stone she grabbed my arm with a grip that I had no idea such a small lady could produce. All I could do was chuckle; it was like a thrill ride. Her comments about the saneness of all Rangers were not very nice.

Greeting me at the airport were Ralph Harter and Rick Ehrler, a couple of the guys I remembered well. It was an incredible feeling to be reunited with those guys, a bit older than I remember, but still good. We sat and talk for a while waiting for Bruce Sartwell to show up. I had heard that Bruce lost all of his Vietnam photos, beret and other memorabilia in a nasty divorce, so I had brought from my home a brand new, made in Vietnam, beret. I had two made after I lost my first one and never had to wear the second one, so I figured that Bruce needed it more than I did. Bruce arrived and he did not look much older than he did in RVN.

The talk and excitement was incredible and I felt more relaxed than any time since I left RVN. We piled into Ralph's car and headed to the Columbus Hilton, the site of the reunion. We checked in and they lost my reservation but Rick said I could room with him until they had a room for me the next day. We put our gear away and decided to meet for a drink and to talk about old times.

Bruce did not drink and Rick, Ralph, and I had very little, but we all came to the conclusion that we had to get the roster of our company in order to find old friends. Bruce volunteered to run for unit director and thus the die was cast. Our old first shirt, Roy Nelson was running for President of the organization and we would contact him later. Later that night we all got together to go to dinner and Ralph brought along his significant other, Sylvia. How Ralph hooked up with this very beautiful southern belle was the question of the evening. After we headed back to our rooms Rick and I talked late into the night. Damn, it was good to be with old friends again. While we had not seen each other in over 24 years it seemed like only yesterday. Hopefully others would feel the same way when we would have our first companywide reunion.

Ralph knocked hard on the door and was ready for breakfast at O'Dark thirty and I had just gotten up. We were anxious to get over to Fort Benning and check out the post and some of the sites around there. It was the 50th Anniversary of the Rangers and there was plenty to do. We had a great time going all over the post and meeting some modern day Rangers. We also viewed where the Ranger Memorial was going to be built. The ground breaking was scheduled for the next afternoon with the Secretary of the Army in attendance. Then we found "Ranger Joes," a store that had all kinds of military surplus. We found all sorts of goodies there and Ralph really made a haul as did Bruce. We all bought t-shirts and had our unit designation printed on the back for the parade the next day. We all agreed to walk and not march, as our marching days were over. We headed back to the hotel for lunch and laughter filled the car, with all taking hits on each other.

After lunch we went to the hospitality room and met up with some others and a number of W W 11 Rangers. We hooked up with Mike Patrick, Top, Woodrow, Nizalek and agreed that we would attend the business meeting the next day and meet for lunch to determine how to proceed to find others. But on that day the ranges were open for us old farts to partake of some of the new firepower these guys had. We all headed to Ralph's car and went back to Fort Benning to do some good old fashion stress relief by burning off as much of the new firepower these guys had. The young Rangers were at each station on the firing line. I sighted an M-60 that was down located in a trench line that had all sorts of nice support and those old man sized silhouettes down range. Rick really wanted to feel the kick of the 60 again and he and I got in line to fire off. Rick is blind and he just wanted to burn off a few rounds for the feel. I took his cane as we got closer and held it behind my back. I guided him with pressure and whispers as he got behind the gun. It was then that I mentioned to the young ranger that Rick was blind and pulled his cane out. The young Ranger asked how he would hit the target and I gave him the cane and instructed him to go down range and tap on the target. While Rick and I got a kick out of his response as he looked at us like he thought we were not kidding. Rick had the weapon shouldered and ready to rock and roll. I told Rick I'd adjust his fire from where I was but, I'm not kidding, he hit the target with the first burst. Incredible, was it luck or fate? The young Ranger could not believe it and the guys on the line gave a big cheer out for Rick. We laughed all the way out of the trench and back to the car. That was it for target practice that day as we did not want to press our luck. The rest of the day we spent hitting Ranger Joe's again and then just talking about all the activity to happen the next day.

First thing up on Saturday was a business meeting and Roy Nelson was running for President of the Association. We had all agreed earlier that Bruce Sartwell would nominate Roy. The business meeting went well and Roy Nelson was elected President of the 75th Ranger Regiment Association Inc. The first of three unit members to serve in this office. Roy invited the members of the unit to lunch and to discuss what we could do to affect a reunion of the company. We discussed many different ideas and ways that we could get a reunion started. Bruce Sartwell was a private detective and had resources; Rick Ehrler had various search devices in his computer and was a computer genius, having learned computer programing, one had access to a national data base of social security numbers. The individual doing that search did it at his own peril of getting into serious trouble at his job and for that reason his name has never been revealed. The vast majority of members were located that way. We knew that we would need to locate old orders that had the social security numbers on them. As we went around the table we found that all of us had a talent that could help us find others. We went thru the unit roster like it was a treasure map finding new and old addresses. That document would be the foundation from which we built our old unit up again. A decision was made to go full throttle and hold the 1st reunion in Baltimore, MD. Part of that decision was due to the closeness of the Vietnam Memorial, something that all wanted to visit.

The year seemed to fly by. We had done well in locating many of the guys and contacting them by phone to set up this reunion. Bruce Sartwell put his money where his mouth was and contracted for a hotel and meeting room by putting it all on a credit card. He really got nervous towards the actual date in hoping that we would be successful. It was exciting as the days grew closer to the day of the reunion. The names of old friends came in as a promise to attend the reunion. Besides finding guys we had been gifted with some items that could be sold to raise a unit fund and get ourselves ready for next reunion. A friend of Ralph bought a gross of coffee cups and mugs with our unit scrolls on them. We sold them to fund future newsletters and reunions. It was incredible the excitement of this 1year mission to reunite was happening. Still the anxiety of, "are we opening a can of worms?" was there. Would it be a success or not?

As the day of the first reunion drew close Bruce Sartwell came up with a brilliant idea. When we visit the Wall we should leave a plaque there listing our fallen comrades and the fact that they were not forgotten. It was decided that we should have two so that one could travel to all the reunions thereafter if we were to still have them. We hoped it would become a tradition that would carry on that special bond that we had with each other. I had a friend who had a trophy business and had been a marine in Vietnam and would do them at cost. Thus with the names we had we created two plaques: one for the wall and one to continue the spirit of our bonds.

I do not remember the trip down to Baltimore but I do remember the emotions running deep. We had taken our motor home down to Baltimore and I just do not remember the trip. When we arrived I remember checking in at the desk and seeing some old familiar faces. How could these guys look so old? I hadn't aged a day in my mind. It was a shock to see so many faces that played such an important time in my life. Shared experiences came rushing at us like flood waters and engulfed us with such joy and sorrow that it was difficult to even breath. We had such deep bonds that no one could describe or understand unless they had been there. It was the start of a great reunion.

I remember seeing guys for the first time in 30 years and guys approaching the hospitality room with hesitation in their eyes. Wondering what kind of a welcome they would get, wondering if any demons from that war would resurface. And to see those concerns melt with smiles and laughter. Damn they were some fine men, and still are. We went to the inner harbor of Baltimore that had been rebuilt and was now prime real estate. Had a great time there and found that the same sense of humor was alive and well. While touring the USS Constitution I was surprised to find out that the cannons were not real and made out of foam. I pointed it out to the wife of one of my closest friends. A couple of real cannons were at the entrance and her husband had tried to lift one. When his wife lifted one in the ship with one hand he was dumfounded. Naturally this brought up who wore the pants in that family. Funny incidents that happened in Vietnam came up from time to time and it was great to find out what other guys thoughts on those incidents were. No one wanted to tell war stories and the time was one of both elation and sadness.

All good times have to end sooner or later as it was with the reunion. We had a great dinner dance the night before we were to leave. Our last act would be to visit the Wall in DC. We had a business meeting on Saturday morning and it was decided we would meet in Las Vegas in two years. A plea was made for all to submit orders that had the Social Security numbers on them so we could continue to find members.

We caravanned to the wall led by Mike Kentes. Mike worked there and was very familiar with the area. We arrived at the wall and set the plaque. Guys were checking for names and it was a time we did not want to end. We managed to get the park police to allow us on the grass for photos with the wall in the background. As we prepared to leave, the guys who worked so hard on getting it going (Barley, Harter, Sartwell, Ehler, Nizalek, and Nelson) agreed that it was a success. Mission accomplished. What was started back in 1992 has continued to grow and prosper with each reunion. *What a* great feeling.

LRRP/RANGERS COMPANY COMMANDERS

CAPTAIN JAMES TEDRICK – NOVEMBER 1966 - APRIL 1967

LT RICK STETSON – APRIL 3 1967 - APRIL 30 1967

LT DONALD LAWRENCE – MAY - JULY 1967

CAPTAIN CLANCY MATSUDA – JULY 1967 - FEBUARY 1968

CAPTAIN DALE DICKEY – FEBUARY 1968 - MAY 1969

CAPTAIN JOHN CONNERS – MAY 1969 - MARCH 1970

CAPTAIN ALBERT ZAPANTA – SEPTEMBER 1969 - MARCH 1970

CAPTAIN GERALD JOHNSON – MARCH 1970 - AUGUST 1970

LT BRENT GULICK – AUGUST 1970 - NOVEMBER 1970

RANGER CREED

Recognizing that I volunteered as a Ranger, fully knowing the hazards of my chosen profession, I will always endeavor to uphold the prestige, honor, and high esprit de corps of my Ranger Regiment.

Acknowledging the fact that a Ranger is a more elite soldier who arrives at the cutting edge of battle by land, sea, or air, I accept the fact that as a Ranger my country expects me to move further, faster and fight harder than any other soldier.

Never shall I fail my comrade. I will always keep myself mentally alert, physically strong and morally straight and I will shoulder more than my share of the task whatever it may be, one hundred-percent and then some.

Gallantly will I show the world that I am a specially selected and well trained soldier. My courtesy to superior officers, neatness of dress and care of equipment shall set the example for others to follow.

Energetically will I meet the enemies of my country. I shall defeat them on the field of battle for I am better trained and will fight with all my might. Surrender is not a Ranger word. I will never leave a fallen comrade to fall into the hands of the enemy and under no circumstances will I ever embarrass my country.

Readily will I display the intestinal fortitude required to fight on to the Ranger objective and complete the mission though I be the lone survivor.

GLOSSARY

AK-47	-	Soviet assault rifle
AO	-	Area of operations
Arc Light	-	B-52 air strike
Arty	-	Artillery
ARVN	-	Army of the Republic of South Vietnam
ATL	-	Assistant team leader
APC	-	Armor troop carrier
Bearcat	-	9th Division Headquarters Base Camp
Berm	-	A wall of dirt used for defense purposes
Bird dog	-	Small fixed wing observation plane
Blasting caps	-	Small device used to trigger the larger main explosive
Break-contact	-	Disengage battle with the enemy
C & C	-	Command and Control
CAR-15	-	Smaller version of the M-16 rifle
Cav.	-	Cavalry
Chicom	-	Chinese Communist
Chopper	-	Helicopter
CIB	-	Combat Infantry Badge
CO	-	Commanding Officer
Cobra	-	Helicopter gunship
CS Grenade	-	Riot Gas
C-4	-	Plastic explosive
DEROS	-	Date of return from overseas duty

Dong Tan	-	9th Division Base camp in the Delta
Doughnut Dollies	-	Female Red Cross Volunteers deployed to Vietnam for a 1 year tour
Duce and a half	-	2 ½ ton Army truck
E & E	-	Escape and Evasion
E Company	-	Unit Designation for the 9th Infantry Division Long Range Patrol. All Ranger units in Vietnam belong to the 75th Infantry Brigade
Extraction	-	Removing a patrol from its area of operation,
Fix	-	Coordinates pertaining to a specific location
FNG	-	Fucking new guy
Frag-grenade	-	Fragmentation grenade often used to break contact with the enemy
G-2	-	Military Intelligence
Gunship	-	Attack Helicopter
H and I	-	Harassment and Interdiction
H E	-	High Explosive
Ho Chi Minh Trail	-	Main supply route from North Vietnam through Laos and Cambodia into South Vietnam
Hooch	-	A small hut or shack
HQ	-	Headquarters
Huey	-	Helicopter
Insertion	-	Placing a team by helicopter or boat where the patrol would start a mission
KIA	-	Killed In Action
LT	-	Lieutenant
LBJ	-	Long Binh Jail (incountry military stockade)
LP	-	Listening post beyond the perimeter to warn of approaching enemy before they attack

LRRP	-	Long Range Recon Patrol, pronounced as "lurp" referred to soldiers specially trained to operate in enemy territory
LRRP Rations	-	lightweight rations carried on patrol made edible by adding water
LZ	-	Landing zone
M-16	-	Standard issue rifle in Vietnam
M-60	-	U. S. Army machine gun
Maguire rig	-	A single rope that hangs from a helicopter with a seat at the end that can hold 3 soldiers while flying at speeds of 90 knots
MIA	-	Missing in action
Mission	-	An operational assignment for a Ranger team
MP	-	Military police
MPC	-	Paper Military money use overseas
NCO	-	Non Commission officer
NVA	-	North Vietnamese Army
Parakeet Mission	-	sudden assaults on the enemy made by Helicopter
PRC-25	-	Standard Issue radio
PRU	-	Vietnamese Mercenary soldiers
PT	-	Physical training
Purple Heart	-	Medal awarded for being wounded in Combat
PX	-	Post Exchange
Radio Relay	-	A method of sending and receiving patrol messages when patrols were too far out to allow regular communications
Rangers	-	LRRPs were designated Rangers after January 31, 1969
Rappel	-	Decent from a helicopter while secured to a rope

R&R	-	Rest and Recuperation, a one week period away from Combat in places such as Bangkok, Hawaii or Japan
SEALs	-	Small Navy Units trained for Special Operations
Short Timer	-	Someone with less than 30 days in country
Sgt.	-	Sergeant
SOP	-	Standard Operating Procedures
Spc-4	-	Specialist Fourth Class
Spider Hole	-	A camouflaged hole with one enemy soldier
Stand Down	-	period of rest between missions
Stay behind	-	A small team that hides while the main unit continues to move through an area
Strobe light	-	Bright flashing light to mark ones position
Team	-	usually a five man patrol designated by a number
TL	-	Team Leader
TOC	-	Tactical or command center
Top	-	Slang for First Sergeant
Tracer	-	ammunition that can be seen at night
VC	-	Viet Cong – South Vietnamese Communist Guerrillas
Web-gear	-	used by rangers to carry equipment such as Canteens, ammunition pouches and bandages
WP	-	Willie Peter -- White Phosphorous grenade